ABOUT THE
STARMONT READER'S GUIDES TO CONTEMPORARY SCIENCE FICTION AND FANTASY AUTHORS

The past two decades have seen an enormous upsurge in the interest in science fiction and fantasy. It is rare to find a bookstore that doesn't now prominently feature brightly colored examples of space and magic. It is unusual to find a high school, college, or university that doesn't offer at least one science fiction or fantasy course. Most significantly, it is becoming increasingly difficult to meet someone who hasn't succumbed to the lure of these two entertaining literatures. The Starmont Reader's Guides were created to satisfy the needs and interests of this varied readership. Bringing together acknowledged authorities, the series offers a thorough examination of each author; indeed, many of these efforts represent the first time the authors have been examined in book form. Each volume is divided into a chronological table of the author's life and literary career, a full biography, chapters on the major works or groups of works, and both primary and secondary bibliographies. Without sacrificing the sophistication that each author creates in his or her fiction, they clearly and cogently explore and explain the important issues, providing depth and understanding for both the beginning and the sophisticated reader.

It is hoped that the Starmont Reader's Guides will be of value to the student, teacher, librarian, scholar and fan by contributing to our understanding of the many authors and fascinating works that have provided us all with so much pleasure and insight.

Dr. Roger C. Schlobin, Series Editor

DR. ROGER C. SCHLOBIN is currently an Associate Professor of English at the North Central Campus of Purdue University. He is co-editor of "The Year's Scholarship in Science Fiction and Fantasy," which appears annually in *Extrapolation;* one of the authors of *A Research Guide to Science Fiction Studies*; and has written *The Literature of Fantasy: An Annotated Bibliography of Fantasy-Fiction* as well as the bibliography of the works of Andre Norton.

ROGER ZELAZNY

STARMONT READER'S GUIDE 2
CARL B. YOKE

Series Editor: ROGER C. SCHLOBIN

BORGO PRESS / WILDSIDE PRESS

www.wildsidepress.com

For Sherry,

Alex,

Chris, and,

of course,

Roger Zelazny

Library of Congress Cataloging in Publication Data

Yoke, Carl B
    The reader's guide to Roger Zelazny.

    (Starmont reader's guides to contemporary
science fiction and fantasy authors)
    Bibliography: p.
    Includes index.
    1. Zelazny, Roger—Criticism and interpretation.
2. Science fiction, American—History and criticism.
I. Title. II. Series.
PS3576.E43Z97   813'.54   79-17107
ISBN 0-916732-04-5

CARL YOKE is currently Assistant to the Vice President at Kent State University, where he is also an Associate Professor of English. He has been a close friend of Roger Zelazny since they shared a desk in the first grade. He has published a variety of poetry and is presently Associate Editor of *Extrapolation*, one of the major science fiction journals.

CONTENTS

ABBREVIATIONS

CC   *The Courts of Chaos.* Garden City, NY: Doubleday and Company, 1978.

DF   *The Doors of His Face, The Lamps of His Mouth and Other Stories.* Garden City, NY: Doubleday and Company, 1971.

DM   *The Dream Master.* New York: Ace Books, 1966.

GA   *The Guns of Avalon.* Garden City, NY: Doubleday and Company, 1972.

LL   *Lord of Light.* Garden City, NY: Doubleday and Company, 1967.

NP   *Nine Princes in Amber.* Garden City, NY: Doubleday and Company, 1970.

RE   "A Rose for Ecclesiastes." In *Four for Tomorrow.* New York: Ace Books, 1973.

TI   *This Immortal.* New York: Ace Books, 1966.

I.

CANON AND CHRONOLOGY

1937   Born in Cleveland, Ohio (May 13).

1943-49   Attends Noble School, Euclid, Ohio; is already writing humorous stories and poems by sixth grade.

1949-52   Attends Shore Junior High School, Euclid, Ohio; continues to develop writing skills through a series of stories called *The Record*; these formative stories are about the Zlaz and Yok monsters, who live in the caves under Paris, sleep for inordinate periods of time, drink great quantities of *zyphoam*, and are always in trouble with their boss because they foul up every assignment they are given, but they luck out in the end; the stories are humorous, full of impossible situations, and involve fairly sophisticated word play.

1952-55   Attends and graduates from Euclid Senior High School, Euclid, Ohio; *The Record* stories continue; Carl Yoke and Dick Covert provide needed feedback for developing ideas.
Takes Journalism course in junior year under Mr. Myron Gordon; becomes news editor for school newspaper in senior year; joins Creative Writing Club under the direction of Mrs. Ruby Olson in junior year; Olson and Gordon encourage writing.

1954   Publishes "Diet," a poem; and "Mr. Fuller's Revolt" and "And the Darkness is Harsh," two short stories in the *Eucuyo*, the school's literary magazine; sells "Mr. Fuller's Revolt" to *Literary Cavalcade*.

1955   Publishes "Slush, Slush, Slush," a poem; and "Youth Eternal" in *Eucuyo*.

1955-59   Attends Western Reserve University, Cleveland, Ohio; decides to be Psychology major, where encounters Freud, Jung, Ellis and the ideas of other theorists; switches to English in junior year; graduates with B. A. in 1959.
Receives letter in fencing; studies judo.

1957   Wins Finley Foster Poetry Prize.

1958   Publishes "The Man Without A Shadow," a poem; and "The Outward Sign," a short story, in the 1958 edition of *Skyline*, the University's literary magazine.

1959   Wins second Finley Foster Prize and the Holden Essay Award.

1959-60   Enrolls at Columbia University for graduate work; spends a great deal of time absorbing New York's cultural assets: the museums, plays, Greenwich Village, small clubs and coffee houses because of interest in folk music.

1960	Leaves New York City to work on Master's Thesis; joins Ohio National Guard; serves six-month tour of active duty, mostly in Texas.
1960-63	Serves Guard obligation first with the 137th Artillery Battalion and then with the 112th Engineers Batallion.
1962	Graduates from Columbia University with M.A. in Elizabethan and Jacobean Drama.

Employed by Social Security Administration, Cleveland, Ohio, as Claims Representative; meets a number of interesting people in this position which help with character development in his writing; learns German on his own.

Publishes first science fiction stories: "Passion Play" and "Horseman" in the August issues of *Amazing* and *Fantastic*, respectively; is encouraged by Cele Goldsmith, the editor of both magazines; publishes "The Teachers Rode a Wheel of Fire" in October issue of *Fantastic* and "Moonless in Byzantium" in December issue of *Amazing*.

1963	Publishes "On the Road to Splenoba," "Final Dining," "The Borgia Hand," "Nine Starships Waiting," "Circe Has Her Problems," "The Malatesta Collection," "Threshold of the Prophet;" "A Museum Piece," "The Misfit," "King Solomon's Ring," and "The Great Slow Kings" in *Amazing*, *Fantastic*, and *New Worlds*; also publishes "The Stainless Steel Leech," "A Thing of Terrible Beauty," "Monologue for Two," and "Mine is the Kingdom" under the pseudonym of Harrison Denmark, a name picked for him by Cele Goldsmith.

Publishes "A Rose for Ecclesiastes" in the July issue of *Fantasy and Science Fiction*; this story produces his first Hugo nomination and draws an enormous amount of attention.

1964	Involved in a very bad automobile accident just outside the Mansfield, Ohio city limits in early Fall.

Because of accident, marriage to Sharon Steberl, scheduled for October 10th, is postponed.

November 25th, Joseph Zelazny, father, dies suddenly.

December 5th, marries Sharon Steberl.

Publishes "The Graveyard Heart," "Collector's Fever," "Lucifer," "The Salvation of Faust," and "The Monster and the Maiden."

1965	Late summer, separates from Sharon Steberl.

Leaves Cleveland for Baltimore when promoted to Claims Policy Specialist.

Publishes "He Who Shapes," "Passage to Dilfar," "The Doors of His Face, the Lamps of His Mouth," "The Furies," "Devil Car," "Thelinde's Song," "Of Time and the Yan," and "But Not the Herald."

"Devil Car" nominated for Hugo.

1966	Wins Hugo for ". . . And Call Me Conrad."
	Divorced from Sharon Steberl, June 27.
	Wins Nebulas for "He Who Shapes" (novella) and "The Doors of His Face, the Lamps of His Mouth" (novelette).
	Publishes *This Immortal* and *The Dream Master*, reworkings of ". . . And Call Me Conrad" and "He Who Shapes" respectively, his first full-length novels.
	Publishes "Love Is An Imaginary Number," "The Bells of Shoredan," "For A Breath I Tarry," "This Moment of the Storm," "The Keys to December," "Divine Light," and "Comes Now the Power."
	Receives Nebula nominations for *This Immortal* (novel), "This Moment of the Storm" (novelette), and "For A Breath I Tarry" (also novelette), and a Hugo nomination for "The Doors of His Face, the Lamps of His Mouth."
	Marries Judith Alene Callahan, August 20.
1967	Publishes *Isle of the Dead, Four for Tomorrow* and *Lord of Light*.
	Publishes "This Mortal Mountain," "Dawn," "Death and the Executioner," "The Man Who Loved the Faioli," "In the House of the Dead," "Angel, Dark Angel," "Damnation Alley," "The Last Inn on the Road," and "Auto-de-Fe."
	Secretary-Treasurer of the Science Fiction Writers of America.
	Receives Nebula nomination for "This Mortal Mountain" (novelette) and "The Keys to December" (novelette), and Hugo nominations for "Comes Now the Power" and "For A Breath I Tarry."
1968	Edits *Nebula Award Stories Three*.
	Wins Hugo for *Lord of Light* (novel).
	Publishes "He That Moves," "Dismal Light," "Song of the Blue Baboon," "Creatures of Light," and "Corrida."
	Receives Hugo nomination for "Damnation Alley" (novella).
1969	Leaves Social Security Administration for full-time writing.
	Publishes "The Steel General," "Creatures of Darkness," "Come to Me Not in Winter's White," "The Year of the Good Seed," and "The Eve of Rumoko."
	Publishes *Creatures of Light and Darkness* and *Damnation Alley*.
	Receives Nebula nomination for *Isle of the Dead*.
1970	Publishes *Nine Princes in Amber*.
1971	Son, Devin, born.
	Publishes "Science Fiction and How It Got That Way" in *The Writer*.
	Publishes *Jack of Shadows* and *The Doors of His Face, the Lamps of His Mouth and Other Stories*.
1972	Publishes *The Guns of Avalon*.

	Isle of the Dead wins the Prix Apollo, French Science Fiction Award.
1973	Publishes " 'Kjwalll'kje'k'koothaill'kje'k."
	Publishes *Today We Choose Faces* and *To Die in Italbar.*
1974	Publishes "The Engine at Heartspring's Center."
	Guest of Honor at the World Science Fiction Convention, Washington, D.C. Collected *Poems* published by DISCON II.
1975	Publishes "The Game of Blood and Dust," "Home is the Hangman," and "Some Science Fiction Parameters: A Biased Opinion."
	Publishes *Sign of the Unicorn* and *Doorways in the Sand,* both in serial.
	Publishes *Sign of the Unicorn* in hardcover.
	Receives Nebula nomination for "The Engine at Heartspring's Center."
	Moves from Baltimore to Santa Fe, New Mexico.
1976	Son, Jonathan Trent, born.
	Publishes *Bridge of Ashes, Doorways in the Sand, The Hand Of Oberon, My Name is Legion,* and *Deus Irae* (with Philip K. Dick).
	Receives Nebula nomination for *Doorways in the Sand*; it is also selected as one of the Best Books for Young Adults by the American Library Association.
	"Home is the Hangman" wins both a Hugo and a Nebula.
1977	Publishes "No Award" in *Saturday Evening Post.*
	Publishes "Is There A Demon Lover in the House."
	The movie version of *Damnation Alley* is released.
	Finishes *The Courts of Chaos,* last of the Amber series.
	The Courts of Chaos, published in serial.

II.

INTRODUCTION

When I think back through the more than thirty years that I have known Roger Zelazny and try to analyze those qualities that make him the great science fiction writer that he is, two things stand out.

First, he is insatiably curious. His appetite for knowledge drives his reading. Though he finds the odd, or the unusual, particularly interesting, he is attracted to any new idea, person, or circumstance. His ability to absorb material is virtually unmatched. It is this quality which makes him difficult to research, for nearly everything he reads turns up eventually in his fiction.

Second, he is a keen student of people. He is extremely sensitive to them, and he meets everyone initially with compassion and sympathy. For him, each individual is a source of new knowledge about man and a possible adventure.

These are not all of the qualities which make the man, of course, but they are those which make the writer. Such curiosity, intelligence, and sensitivity can produce many effects: alienation, vanity, snobbishness, and boorishness, and honestly, I have seen all of these qualities in Zelazny at times. But, because he has experienced these states of mind himself and understands them, he can accurately draw characters who display them.

Zelazny, today, is a mature adult who is gentle, loving, and understanding. He retains the ability to laugh at life and himself. He loves life and people and is basically optimistic. Like many of his principle characters, he has metamorphosed beyond the small and the petty.

Zelazny's life can be broken down into three broad but distinguishable phases. The first of these runs from his birth on May 13, 1937, in Cleveland, Ohio, through the publication of his first stories in 1962. It may be described as formative, and it is basically educational. Yet, most of the major ideas that later show up in his published stories were born at this time.

Zelazny attended Noble Elementary School in Euclid, Ohio, from 1943 to 1949. It was there that I first met him. He was a bright but undisciplined student. By the time he reached sixth grade, he was already writing humorous stories about monsters and fabulous creatures, who were a great deal more sympathetic than some of his teachers.

From 1949 to 1955, he attended Shore Junior High and Euclid Senior High Schools. There, he encountered many of the ideas and developed many of the skills which were to appear later. In particular, he began to write a series of stories collectively called *The Record*, about two monster agents who lived under Paris in the catacombs; drank far too much *zyphoam*, an alcoholic beverage; slept for inordinate periods of time, and were always in trouble with their boss. He would send them on a mission only in desperation, and they would inevitably foul it up. However, their colossal luck always allowed them to accomplish something else in the process. A huge, petrified dinosaur, for example, gets buried and becomes the Rocky Mountains. How it got that way, of course, is the story. In general, these stories are marked by humor, impossible situations, and sophisticated word play. More importantly, they gave Zelazny an opportunity to exercise his imagination, and the structuring of their mythologies taught him to discipline his mind and his evolving skills.

During that period, several people influenced him. Dick Covert, another close friend, and I served as sounding boards for his ideas. Two teachers, Ruby Olson and Myron Gordon, in Creative Writing and Journalism respectively, gave him the positive feedback that he needed to continue developing, and the sale of a short story titled, "Mr. Fuller's Revolt," to *Literary Cavalcade* in 1954 was yet another source of encouragement.

In 1955, Zelazny enrolled at Western Reserve University in Cleveland. At first, he majored in Psychology, where he became formally acquainted with Freud, Jung, Ellis, and other theorists. Then, discouraged by the inconsistencies in the field and encouraged by his successes at writing, he switched to English. In 1957 he won the University's Finley Foster Poetry Prize, and in 1959 he won the prize again as well as the Holden Essay Award for an expanded term paper on Chaucer. Here began his formal acquaintance with Mann, Rilke, the French Symbolist poets, Shakespeare, Whitman, Harte Crane and others, though as with the psychologists, he was already familiar with much of their work. During his undergraduate years, he also learned fencing and judo.

Though he was still writing science fiction stories during this period, most of his time was given over to serious poetry. The product of that effort was a collection of poems called *Chisel in the Sky*. Now cannibalized, 66 poems still remain in the collection, most of which have never been published.

In the Fall of 1959, Zelazny entered Columbia University. During that year or so that he spent in New York, he devoured the city's theaters, museums, and Greenwich Village clubs and coffee houses because of his interest in folk music. In 1960, he left New York to work on his Master's Thesis in Elizabethan and Jacobean drama. Later that year, he joined the Ohio National Guard, spending the bulk of his six-month tour of active duty in Texas. It was after he returned from that tour that he wrote "A Rose For Ecclesiastes."

He then finished his Master's Thesis and, in 1962, got a job with the Social Security Administration in Cleveland as a Claims Representative. In August of that year, his first two stories appeared in *Amazing* and *Fantastic*.

The second phase of Zelazny's development as a writer runs from this time until late 1969. It is marked by great highs and lows in his life. Most of the highs involved his writing. He won two Hugos and two Nebulas during this period and was nominated for these awards seventeen times. His lows included the death of his father, Joseph, in 1964; a disastrous automobile accident just outside the city limits of Mansfield, Ohio, also in 1964; and a divorce from Sharon Steberl, his first wife, in mid-1966.

In 1965, Zelazny left the Cleveland area for Baltimore because he had been promoted to the central office of Social Security. There, he met Judy Callahan, whom he married in 1966. She brought not only a great deal of love but a great deal of stability to his life.

He published his first novels during this time, became well-acquainted with most of his contemporaries, and rose to great standing in the field. Then, in 1969, he quit his job with Social Security and began writing full-time, a move which he had contemplated for at least two years. Though he had been reading science and mathematics for some time, his interests were intensified when some medical problems gave increased free time to read.

The third phase of Zelazny's development begins at about this time, though it is difficult to date it exactly. It is marked by almost full-time novel writing, a more realistic, less optimistic point of view, and a great deal more stability and security. As much as anything, the realization that he could make a living by writing full-time brought this about.

More science enters his stories during this phase, and his style manifests control. Though there are some Hugo and Nebula nominations and the Prix Apollo in 1972, it is not until 1976 that "Home is the Hangman" brought him both prizes again.

His personal life is marked by the birth of his first son, Devin, in 1971; his second, Jonathan Trent, in 1976; and his move from Baltimore to Santa Fe, New Mexico, in 1975.

Most recently, there have been three significant achievements. First, he published "No Award" in the *Saturday Evening Post*. Second, the movie version of *Damnation Alley* was released, and though the movie bore little resemblance to the novel, it has opened up possibilities for other movie sales. Third, he has finished the last Amber novel, *The Courts of Chaos*, which will surely bring him acclaim as a fantasist.

Themes

There are several recurrent themes in Zelazny's fiction: immortality, love, vanity, fertility, guilt, sacrifice, suicide, revenge, power. Like life itself, however, they are integrated into patterns which delineate specific pictures of man himself. For example, vanity or guilt often blocks a person's growth. They prevent his experience from transforming him into a mature individual. Unless he is transformed, he cannot enter into a psychologically healthy love relationship or make an unselfish sacrifice. Such transformations can only come from the impact of a traumatic experience, which causes a rebalancing of personality and breaks down neurosis. Fertility is a metaphor for this same process in its broader sense of restoration. Immortality provides the individual extended opportunities to accumulate experience and therefore to continue to grow so that he can perform those tasks necessary to save the world, the universe, a doomed race, or to perform some other bigger-than-life task.

These themes are usually projected against a philosophical background constituted by two perpetually opposed forces, form and chaos, which are interdependent and ever working to create change. The cycle creates a rhythm in the universe which permeates all things. Man, or other intelligent creatures, may alter that rhythm by will or self-discipline, but only in time or degree. Form and chaos themselves are amoral. Either may be good or bad depending upon the circumstances or the point of view. Moral judgments are made by intelligent creatures.

Zelazny's themes are the stuff of which life is made. They cover the range of human experience, but they are treated freshly in imaginative contexts. They generally present a positive view about life and about man, and even when the characters die, they have usually achieved something of significance, something of lasting or greater value, such as Jarry Dark does in "The Keys to December." The themes ring true to human experience, and though cast in exotic settings, they are both universal and contemporary.

Characters

That Zelazny's principal characters owe their origin to Northrop Frye is no secret. He has stated on many occasions that his heroes fall into what Frye defines as the "high mimetic mode." That is, a hero who is ". . . superior in degree to other men but not to his natural environment . . . . He has authority, passions, and powers of expression far greater than ours, but what he does is subject to both social criticism and the order of nature." (1)

Zelazny's principal characters are always larger-than-life. His heroes are often immortal or near-immortal, stronger, taller, and more intelligent than normal men. Because of this, they have often been alienated from their societies and, as a result, are rebels of one kind or another. If they are not labeled rebels, like Hell Tanner of *Damnation Alley*, then they have been rebels at some previous time and are currently co-existing with society. Often, they are forced to save that society as part of solving their own psychological dilemmas.

Zelazny's women, especially the hero's love-object and his villains, are also larger-than-life in some way. Jean Luharich in "The Doors of His Face, the Lamps of His Mouth" and Kali/Brahma in *Lord of Light* are such women. The antagonists, too, fit the definition. Logically, both the women and the villians must be worthy of the hero's attention. The tension in the story can only come if the antagonist is of equal or nearly equal size to the hero.

These characteristics, of course, give the principal characters near-god status, which Zelazny reinforces quite often by associating them with the gods of mythology or the heroes of legend. The clustering of numerous hero or godly identities about the protagonist give him definition and dimension.

Balanced against the physical proportions of these characters are their realistic human qualities. Psychologically, they are entirely credible. They not only could exist, they do. Moreover, it is their very humanness which triggers the psychological and physical quests that they undertake.

The acts that they perform are completely in keeping with their make-ups, and their motivations are the standard human motivations: greed, revenge, love, power. They are mostly men-of-action, and the events that constitute the plots derive naturally and logically from the structure of their personalities.

Zelazny's heroes usually reveal themselves during the course of the story by their dialogue, thoughts, and actions. Since he frequently writes in the first person, the other characters reveal themselves through the same techniques. Each of the principal characters is fully-developed, and we are presented a composite picture of their psychological, physical, and emotional qualities.

The conflict between the hero and antagonist often represents the larger universal conflict between form and chaos with its corollary conflict between good and evil. Sometimes the hero and the villain are virtually mirror-images of one another, and it is their different levels of maturity or their differences in point of view that bring them into conflict. Occasionally, the villian is simply mad.

Accompanying the external conflict in the story, there is frequently an internal conflict to be resolved in the hero. He is usually neurotic, and this neurosis must be overcome for him to achieve his physical goal. At very least, he must grow a great deal to succeed; though in some cases, he does not. If he does not, then, like Charles Render in *The Dream Master*, he is committed to some form of madness. Growth is the means that Zelazny chooses to show his characters changing, and that growth is produced by the impact of his experience. Nearly always, growth is of such large degree that it can be termed metamorphic.

Though many of the minor characters are no more than foils, some are brilliant sketches. Vialle, the blind sculptress in the Amber novels, is an example. With a deftness that is indeed amazing, Zelazny is able to give his minor figures dimension that less capable writers spend an entire story developing. Often he does it in a single short scene.

Plots

In a work of this kind, a detailed analysis of Zelazny's plots is prohibitive. However, several general comments can be made about them.

First, most of Zelazny's plots follow the classic mold with a definite beginning, middle, and end; a conflict to be resolved; a climax; and a resolution. Often, to create interest, he will begin his story by lifting a piece of action from somewhere near the end and placing it at the beginning. *Lord of Light*, for example, begins with what would be placed between books vi and vii if the story were progressing in strict chronological order. "Home Is The Hangman" follows the same pattern, lifting the material which would immediately precede the climax and placing it at the outset of the story.

Second, when he does not do this, he often begins his stories by introducing the reader to a character who is seriously disoriented, who is out of his natural place and time, or who is searching for his identity. (2) Corwin. the protagonist of the Amber series, is an excellent example of this. From either of these two beginnings, there is a period of development and explanation, a low in the pacing, in other words, which allows Zelazny to explain how his character got into the situation in the first place. The heroes are inevitably on a quest of some kind with some physical object in mind. Sam is trying to overthrow the gods in *Lord of Light*, Corwin is trying to save the kingdom in the Amber series, Davits is trying to capture an Ikky in "The Doors of His Face, the Lamps of His Mouth," and so on. Inevitably, however, the physical quest is paralleled by a psychological one. The characters are trying to re-balance their own personalities.

Third, after overcoming several obstacles, there is eventually a confrontation between the hero and his chief resistance. Often the resistance is another intelligent being who represents his "Moriarity." In other words, he is an opponent of almost equal powers. The two represent good and evil, light and dark, form and chaos. Sandow encounters Belion in *Isle of the Dead*, Corwin encounters Brand, Davits encounters the Ikky. Sometimes the hero himself defeats his adversary; at other times, someone else does but the hero has been responsible for making the defeat possible. It is not Corwin who kills Brand, Davits who finally catches the first Ikky, or Sam who destroys Kali/Brahma. Nonetheless, the protagonist triumphs, and in triumphing, he undergoes a metamorphosis of personality. Though the physical victory may not be his directly, the psychological one certainly is.

Fourth, the resolution is often open-ended. The hero either pushes off for new experiences or is about to. He is always armed, however, with a new maturity which will enable him to continue to grow.

Fifth, both the conflicts and the action in Zelazny stories occur at two levels: the physical and psychological. The achievement of the physical goal also represents the achievement of the phychological goal. Again, the capture of Ikky is also the conquest of Davits' neurosis; the defeat of Chaos is also the mark of Corwin's maturity. Sometimes, the hero fails. Render does not defeat Thaumiel of Qliphoth in *The Dream Master*, and he also loses the psychological battle. And though the plot actions may not be realistic from the physical point of view, they are from the psychological.

Sixth, the plots are often organized along the lines of a Grail quest and incorporate elements from that motif. The actions of the plot broadly follow those from the quest or from some other mythological source. Sometimes, they are taken or developed from the Bible or Shakespeare.

Finally, they are always organic to the basic purpose of the story and develop logically out of the substance of human motivation.

Style

Not with a whimper but a bang. That is how Zelazny's writing career began. When he exploded on the science fiction scene in 1962, the fallout was a shower of simile, symbol, and allusion. Images fresh and new burst in fields of varigated color. Rich tapestries full of mythic characters and beasts unfolded in poetic escapes from reality. He rose, he flew, he soared. Powerful sometimes, gentle at others, he raged and he wept, he bled and he healed, he restored and he destroyed. But always he did it with style.

Never simple and clear-cut, always complex, involved, and difficult, his early style was nonetheless graceful and richly suggestive. It was distinctive. It brought to bear all that he had read, all that he knew. It was the man.

Several things stand out in that early style. One of these is his use of symbols. Drawing on his vast store of Jungian psychology, Zelazny's characters are often archetypes. These original models of the collective unconscious after which similar things are patterned were symbols in themselves. A partial list of those identified and described by Jung sounds remarkably familiar: birth, rebirth, death, power, magic, the hero, the child, the trickster, God, the demon, the wise old man, the earth mother, the giant. (3) Zelazny adopted some, and adapted others. Often he tips off the reader to the symbolic value of the character by using character-names which represent that value. Mahasamatman (*Lord of Light*), for example, means "great souled one," Render (*The Dream Master*), means to "make or form," and Davits means "curved uprights of timber or iron, projecting over the stern or sides of a vessel, which are used for suspending or hoisting a small boat."

Moreover, the principal characters are often symbols for the forces of form and chaos, and/or good and evil. The hero is a symbol of form and/or good, and the villain, a symbol of chaos and/or evil. Sam in *Lord of Light* and Corwin in the Amber series, for example, represent form and good, while Yama and Kali/Brahma in *Lord of Light* and Corwin's antagonist Brand represent chaos and evil. Two things must be noted. First, form and good are *not* synonymous terms. Neither are chaos and evil. Second, each person contains both form and chaos within himself and will be both creative and destructive during his lifetime. Because of the pendulum effect between these two forces, however, at any particular place or point in time, one or the other will hold dominance.

In addition to his character symbols, Zelazny also creates several recurring symbols in his fiction. Besides the character-symbols representing form and chaos, two of the most prevalent are the rose and the dance. In general, the rose is a symbol of transformation, either of personality or relationship. The dance is a symbol of order and the rhythmic interplay between form and chaos.

One of the important techniques that Zelazny uses in creating symbols is to cluster various images around a central, more general concept. For example, in "The Doors of His Face, the Lamps of His Mouth," he loads a section of the story with images that all have to do with water: the sea, rain, a brook, tears, dew, and ice. In this particular case, the water images pattern to create a symbol which stands for the randomness of life. Another example of this technique occurs in *The Dream Master* where images of snow, cold, ice, white, and flakes pattern to stand for winter, and winter to Render represents death. These patterned symbols are quite common in Zelazny's work and are indicative of his complexity.

In general, his symbols are rarely simple. Often they have multiple meanings which are relevant to the various levels of the story and sometimes they are combined to increase their richness.

The ring symbol in "The Doors of His Face, the Lamps of His Mouth" is an example of how a symbol may have multiple meanings. It appears at the end of the novelette in the form of the planet Saturn. Rings because of their shape traditionally imply union or completeness, but they are also symbolic of marriage. Moreover, in the context of the story, they tie in with Zelazny's other circle symbols because of their shape. The circle symbols, or *mandalas*, stand for psychological completeness in the story. An example of combining symbols occurs in "A Rose for Ecclesiastes": Braxa is a symbolic rose and also the ultimate dancer, bringing together the symbols of transformation and order. A second example of this occurs in the Amber novels in the form of Corwin's emblem, the silver rose. Here, again, two symbols are being combined into one. The rose, again, is a symbol of transformation, and silver is a symbol of power over evil.

Another aspect of Zelazny's early style is his abundant use of myth and legend. Often it is used to structure his stories, sometimes it is used to provide symbols, and at other times, it gives a deeper, richer, and broader meaning to them. The use of the grail myth and other Arthurian lore in the Amber novels helps to structure the events of the plot. The figurative descents to hell in "The Doors of His Face, the Lamps of His Mouth" and *This Immortal* become important symbols for the interpretation of those works. The "Tristan" and "Lady of the Lake" lore in *The Dream Master* most decidedly broaden and deepen the meaning of the theme.

His early work too, is full of humor, and it comes in many forms. There are numerous examples of word play, frequently as puns. In "Dawn," an excerpt from *Lord of Light*, Zelazny writes, "Then, the fit hit the Shan." Unfortunately, the humor does not always work. Sometimes, as in "Dawn," it "shatters the general tone." (4)

Zelazny's early style is also marked by an abundance of devices which are generally regarded as poetic. He showers us with metaphors, similes, personifications, and colorful imagery, for example. In each instance, his usage is fresh and crisp, reflecting both the breadth and depth of his mind. Some of his metaphors and similes are particularly striking, as "The impression of moonlight on a hundred lakes: coins at a dark pool's bottom" from *Isle of the Dead*. And though his allusions are often frustrating and distracting, they do further the purpose of the work by adding to the scope of the principal characters or expanding their themes.

Zelazny's imagery is poetically distinctive. His style is dominated by color images and images of polarity, and although there is a general impression of rose and amber in his work, he uses other colors with the deftness of a painter to suggest the emotional feel of the story. The gray, black, and white images of *The Dream Master*, for example, not only influence the reader's reaction but foreshadow the outcome of the book. Similarly, the images of polarity in *Lord of Light* mirror the basic conflict between form and chaos.

And, a close analysis of his lines, particularly in his descriptive passages, reveals such other poetic devices as alliteration, assonance, consonance, and rhythm. Particularly striking is his use of verbs in such examples as " . . . is pearled by a glowing light to my left" and "Sounds dopplered from dark smears . . . ," both from *The Courts of Chaos*. The last example is particularly interesting because it mixes the sound and sight senses in a phenomenon known in Psychology as synesthesia.

This, then, is but a brief summary of those qualities which mark Zelazny's style. The differences between the early style and that which emerges in the late '60s is not so much one of quality and substance as it is one of quantity and degree. In the later period, there is less of the poetic quality, but there is much greater control.

1. Northrop Frye, *Anatomy of Criticism* (Princeton, NJ: Princeton University Press, 1973), p. 34.
2. Joseph Sanders, "Zelazny: Unfinished Business," in *Voices for the Future*, ed. Thomas D. Clareson (Bowling Green, OH: Bowling Green University Popular Press, 1978), II, 5.
3. Calvin S. Hall and Vernon J. Nordby, *A Primer of Jungian Psychology* (New York: Mentor Books, 1973), p. 41.
4. Banks Mebane, "Gunfire i' the Court, Wildfire at Midnight," *Algol*, 5, No. 13 (1968), 43.

III.

A ROSE FOR ECCLESIASTES

"A Rose For Ecclesiastes," one of Roger Zelazny's earliest published novelettes, clearly establishes the pattern of writing which was to sky-rocket him to the pinnacle of the science fiction profession. Its themes of love, vanity, and fertility; its references to the Bible, poetry, and drama; its mythic quality; its explosion of rich imagery; its symbols of the rose and the dance; its humanness; and its ever-present and often frustrating allusions were to become the hallmarks of his early works.

Though the novelette was published in the November, 1963, issue of the *Magazine of Fantasy and Science Fiction*, Zelazny has acknowledged that it was written nearly two years before. His hesitation in submitting it for publication came "because he knew that the Mars of its setting had lost all credibility by 1962." (1) Despite this fault, however, the story was an immediate success and has continued to be one of his most popular. Though it received neither a Hugo nor a Nebula, it was selected as one of the most outstanding novelettes of the early sixties by the Science Fiction Writers of America and included in *The Science Fiction Hall of Fame*.

The story is about Gallinger, a conceited poet with an almost legendary ability with languages, who comes to Mars to translate the sacred books of the Martian civilization. There he meets a beautiful dancer named Braxa, and he soon falls in love with her. She seduces him and becomes pregnant. The Martian males are sterile, so Braxa's pregnancy causes much elation. Shortly thereafter though, Braxa disappears, and he begins searching frantically for her. He finds out that both she and the baby have been doomed to death by the ruling Mothers because the birth of the child would violate the teachings of their sacred books. Gallinger refuses to accept their decision. Instead, he forces new life on Mars by showing M'Cwyie, the Head Priestess, and the other Mothers a rose. It is a form of life that they have never seen before, and this fulfills an ancient Martian prophecy. Because of this, Braxa and the child are permitted to live, and racial suicide is avoided. Though he has saved the Martians, however, Gallinger learns that Braxa does not love him and never has. She was only trying to fulfill the prophecy by conceiving his child. Shattered, he tries to commit suicide by taking an overdose of sleeping pills. He fails, and wakes up in the ship's dispensary on his way home to Earth.

Of course, a plot summary cannot depict the emotional impact of the story. That comes from the successful interweaving of the story elements and the proper development of its themes.

In "A Rose for Ecclesiastes," a great part of the emotional impact is conveyed by the theme of "betrayed love," even though that is not the primary purpose of the story. Love is one of the many recurrent Zelazny themes and usually fulfills one of two purposes. First, it is often used as a central experience in carrying out Zelazny's belief that man must experience all that he possibly can. This is the point of life. Love teaches man about the most important subject he can study—man himself. Healthy love forms a large part of his ever-optimistic and eternally human view of the world.

Occasionally love is the central purpose of Zelazny's stories, but usually it is a predominant supporter of the main theme. In "A Rose for Ecclesiastes," Gallinger's love for Braxa produces her pregnancy and that, in turn, causes the eventual salvation of the Martian race. It thus supports the story's primary theme, the restoration of fertility.

Second, love has the capability to transform the personalities of one or both of the lovers. It promotes individual growth. Whether or not the affair ends happily, psychological development is inevitable. This is true of Gallinger. Even Emory, the Project Head, notices it. " 'You have been behaving differently these past couple of months . . . I couldn't help wondering what was happening. I didn't know anything mattered that strongly to you.' " (RE, p. 203). It does matter, of course. The depth of his involvement with Braxa is indicated by the fact that he tries to commit suicide when he learns that the affair is over.

Regardless of its outcome, however, Gallinger's affair has transformed him. He has learned humility. Though he has justified his vanity up to this point by rationalizing it with the acclaim he has received on Earth for his poetic and linguistic genius, the experience of love has forced his maturity.

This change cannot come about without a realization of the problem. Gallinger does become aware of his vanity through his relationship with Braxa. He reveals this in his response to M'Cwyie's remark that he is a holy man. " 'I'm not . . . just a second-rate poet with a bad case of hubris.' " (RE, p. 214).

As indicated earlier, the main theme of this story is not love, but fertility. This is indicated in the surface level of the work and is supported by Zelazny's use of the "dying and reviving god" model identified by Sir James G. Frazer in his *Golden Bough*. These gods give up their lives to restore fertility to the land. Then, after spending several months in the underworld, they are re-born. Anthropomorphic representations of the changing seasons, they were believed to assure the annual growth of the crops by their symbolic death and rebirth. Though Zelazny makes no attempt to link Gallinger directly with Tammuz, Adonis, Osiris, and the other gods of the model, he does create the prototypic myth in the story. Gallinger, the conceited rhymer, does symbolically die, and his death guarantees Martian survival by bringing them the one thing they cannot provide for themselves—fertility. Not only will the race be restored but so too will the land because M'Cwyie promises that they will try to grow flowers (RE, p. 215). Further evidence of the "dying and reviving god" model is found in the fact that Braxa disappears for a time as the lovers of the fertility gods are apt to do in the old myths.

Depth and significance are added to the restoration theme by the complex symbolism of the rose itself. In general, it signifies transformation. The key to its interpretation is found in the story's title, "A Rose for Ecclesiastes."

23

Ecclesiastes is noted for its persistent pessimism and its insistence that all is vanity. Each of these is presented as a problem in Zelazny's novelette. The Martians suffer from extreme pessimism, and Gallinger, as has already been established, suffers from vanity. Its result is to block his growth as a person, thus preventing his healthy psychological development and prohibiting him from understanding. Specifically, it occludes his ability to see things clearly. He makes statements to this effect twice in the story. First, in response to M'Cwyie's remark that their city goes far back into the mountain, he says, " 'I see,' I said, seeing nothing" (RE, p. 177). Then at another time, he refers to himself as "Samson in Gaza," in other words, a man who is blind (RE, p. 215).

Like Gallinger's vanity, the fierce Martian pessimism blocks their growth, inhibits their thinking, obscures their vision. When Gallinger suggests, for example, that they might try mating with Earthmen, M'Cwyie rejects the idea, even though it would save their race. So strong is their pessimistic acceptance of the doctrines of the sacred books that when they learn that Braxa is pregnant, they condemn both her and the unborn child to death. It is only because Gallinger accidentally fulfills the prophecy by smashing the Fist of Malann, the giant temple guard, and showing them something new—the rose—that they reverse their decision. M'Cwyie admits that their vision had been blocked when she remarks, " 'You read us his words, as great as Locar's. You read us how there is " ' "nothing new under the sun." ' " And you mocked his words as you read them—showing us a new thing' " (RE, p. 174).

For each of these problems, Zelazny offers a solution in the form of a rose. For the Martian pessimism, he offers a real rose, a red American Beauty, grown in the hydroponics lab by Kane. That rose became the focus of the Mothers' attention (RE, p. 212). It transforms their pessimism to optimism, brings them new life, saves their race.

For Gallinger's vanity, he offers a rose in the form of Braxa. That we are to interpret her this way is confirmed by several clues. First, Gallinger actually compares her to one when he shows her the rose from the hydroponics lab (RE, p. 217). Second, she is described in rose colors. "Her red cloak matched her hair and lips, so perfectly, and those lips were trembling. . . . They were jade, her eyes" (RE, p. 194). Finally, after seeing Braxa perform the one-hundred-seventeenth dance of Locar, Gallinger writes a poem about a rose and calls it "Braxa." It is the metaphoric rose that destroys Gallinger's vanity when she rejects his love, and it is clear that in the future the impact of that experience will make him a different person.

The meaning of the rose symbol is complicated by Gallinger's reference to Blake's sick rose, just after witnessing Braxa's sacred dance. To understand what Zelazny means by the allusion, it is first necessary to explain that Blake's poem is about the transformation from innocence to experience and that it has sexual overtones. (2)

In the context of the story, the "sick rose" has a double meaning because it has two references. Braxa is one of these, and in her case, the term "sick" simply foreshadows what is about to happen. Her sexual encounter with Gallinger will produce a pregnancy and that, in turn, will lead to a death sentence. So, at that point in the story, her figurative loss of innocence would appear to mean her death.

But the poem that Gallinger writes not only refers to Braxa as an individual, it also implies the Martian race as a whole. So, the second meaning of the "sick rose" reference must apply to them. In that context, it also makes sense, for they are "sick" because they are infertile and thus dying.

To make ultimate sense of the reference, however, requires that it be viewed from a broader perspective. This comes from Zelazny's positive view of experience. He does not see it as negative or abnormal, in contrast to the connotation of the word "sick." The loss of innocence is, rather, a natural part of human growth and development, and he welcomes it as the ultimate stimulus for psychological evolution.

It is very likely that the rose symbol came initially from Rilke. Several clues in the story indicate this. First, Gallinger reads Rilke's poetry to Braxa so often that she comes to believe that he is Rilke. Second, he nearly comes to believe it himself and even imagines himself in the Castle Duino writing the *Elegies.* Third, he quotes a passage from the "First Elegy" which expresses how strange it is to be dead and no longer able to interpret roses. At one point, overwhelmed with a sense of things passing, Gallinger remarks, "No! Never interpret roses! Don't. Smell them . . . pick them, enjoy them. Live in the moment. Hold to it tightly. But charge not the gods to explain. So fast the leaves go by, are blown . . . " (RE, p. 198). It is obvious that he senses that his relationship with Braxa is changing, is passing, but he does not want to believe that it will end.

The implication of the allusion from the "First Elegy" is that Gallinger will die figuratively when the transformation process begins and that will be triggered by the dying relationship.

Further evidence that the rose symbol was taken from Rilke comes from the poet's belief that roses not only possess the capability to transform but also to resolve those contradictions which are so much a part of life. Rilke recognized that paradoxes were at the heart of all things, especially miracles, but came to believe that they sprang from the primordial source of all being. They only seemed to be paradoxes because man lacked complete insight. (3)

This is exactly the same conclusion that Gallinger comes to in his final discussion with M'Cwyie. When she refers to him as a "holy man" and says that the Martians will never forget his teachings, he replies,

> "Don't," I said, automatically, suddenly knowing the great paradox which lies at the heart of all miracles. I did not believe a word of my own gospel, never had (RE, p. 215).

A moment later that perception is reinforced, when Gallinger thinks to himself, "*I have conquered thee, Malann—and the victory is thine . . . God damned*" (RE, p. 215).

Zelazny's debt to Rilke goes beyond his appropriation of the rose as

25

a symbol of transformation, however, for he also adopts the poet's other symbol for transformation—the dance.

In *Ranier Maria Rilke: Masks and the Man*, H. F. Peters identifies the significance of the dance in his analysis of the poet's "Sonnets to Orpheus":

> In Orpheus . . . he [Rilke] had found the symbol for the continuous transformation of the world into rhythmic vibrations; and in the figure of the dancer, both an illustration of that process and the assurance that at the highest level the dichotomy between art and life is resolved. (4)

Rilke's concepts of the dance are drawn from the French poet, Paul Valery, who expresses the idea that the dance is transformation, that it is an act of pure metamorphosis, that its rhythm reveals the essence of things, and that through it we get insight into the meaning of existence. (5)

Rilke, himself, comes eventually to the belief that the individual must pursue the course of self-fulfillment and not that of self-surrender and that this can be accomplished by fully achieving our identities rather than losing them. In the dancer, he sees such transcendence. For him, the dancer attains complete self-expression and complete self-surrender. (6)

Zelazny mirrors these ideas. Braxa is the ultimate dancer, and in her, he has created a double symbol of transformation, since she is also the metaphoric rose. This fact permits a projection of Gallinger's psychological development, even though when the story ends, he is in a state of great depression. By analogy, he becomes Orpheus and Braxa becomes Eurydice. In analyzing the metamorphic process found in the "Sonnets," Peters comments:

> Again we are urged to anticipate the end: death, the winter of life, the last farewell—to anticipate it as Orpheus anticipated it when he "died in Eurydice." Her departure, which went through the center of his heart, made him the "singing god," the transformer of death. "To be dead in Eurydice" means to have made one beloved person, whose death was our death, an element in our life; to have impressed our grief so deeply upon our heart that it burst into song. (7)

Though Zelazny has changed the circumstances to fit his story, the pattern is basically the same in the relationship between Gallinger and Braxa. Like Orpheus, Gallinger dies, but it is a figurative rather than literal death. Like Eurydice, Braxa is also dead, but it is in the sense that she never loved him in the first place. She conducted the affair with him because she thought it was her duty.

Moreover, his love impels him to burst into song. He writes a poem to her. The end result of all this is, of course, that Gallinger transforms like Orpheus. Specifically, like the god is reborn, so shall Gallinger be figuratively reborn.

For Zelazny, the Rilkean concept of dance was reinforced by that of Havelock Ellis, a psychologist whose writings were very familiar to him. In *The Dance of Life*, Zelazny finds the connection between the dance and his own form and chaos philosophy. In comparing life to a dance, Ellis writes:

> The dance is the rule of number and of rhythm and of measure and of order, of the controlling influence of form, or the subordination of the parts to the whole. That is what a dance is. And these same properties also make up the classic spirit, not only in life, but, still more clearly and definitely in the universe itself. We are strictly correct when we regard not only life but the universe as a dance. For the universe is made up of a certain number of elements, less than a hundred, and the "periodic law" of these elements is metrical. They are ranged, that is to say, not haphazardly, not in groups, but by number, and those of like quality appear at fixed and regular intervals. Thus our world is, even fundamentally, a dance, a single metrical stanza in a poem which will be forever hidden from us. . . . (8)

It is clear that from Ellis, Zelazny drew the idea of dance as a symbol of some hidden but universal rhythm and of dance as the controlling influence of form.

As with most of his stories, Zelazny's form and chaos philosophy provides the conceptual substructure for "A Rose for Ecclesiastes." The Martian society is an example of form carried to such an extreme that it has become inhibitive.

Betty first makes Gallinger aware of the Martian concern for form when she introduces him to M'Cwyie. She says, " 'Do not forget their Eleven Forms of Politeness and Degree. They take matters of form quite seriously,' " and " 'She [M'Cwyie] expects you to observe certain rituals in handling them [the Martian Sacred Books] like repeating the sacred words when you turn pages—she will teach you the system' " (RE, p. 174). This idea is reinforced for him when Gallinger finds out that there are two thousand, two hundred and twenty-four dances of Locar; that each is highly structured; and that Braxa knows them all. From his translating, he learns that the Martians believe that movement is the first law of life and that the dance is the only legitimate reply to the inorganic (RE, p. 181). Finally, their society is so structured that when Gallinger tells Braxa that their child will prove that the races can inter-marry and that this will save the Martians from extinction, she replies, " 'You have read the Book of Locar . . . Death was decided, voted upon, and passed, shortly after it appeared in this form. But long before, the followers of Locar knew. They decided it long ago. " ' "We have done all things," they said, "we have seen all things, we have heard and felt all things. The dance was good. Now let it end" ' " (RE, p. 207). The repressiveness is obvious from this statement. Locar has already decided all things, so why try to change them. Form has prevented the Martians from even saving themselves.

In Zelazny's philosophy, neither form nor chaos is permitted to dominate indefinitely. Sooner or later, the subordinate force will take control. This rhythmic process continues endlessly, swinging first to one pole and then the other.

It is, therefore, predictable that where form has operated to such a degree that everything has become static chaos will eventually intrude. This is exactly what happens. In both Gallinger and Braxa, Zelazny has created instruments of destruction.

Through the hydroponically grown rose, Martian pessimism is destroyed, and through Braxa, the metaphoric rose, the self-assured and arrogant Gallinger at the outset of the story is destroyed.

But Zelazny also believes that in all individuals is also the capability for reformation, so we also find in both characters the seed for re-creation. Gallinger provides the Martians with fertility which will insure their continued existence. Braxa's rejection, on the other hand, provides Gallinger with humility, the element necessary for the re-formation of his personality.

The capability for both destruction and creation is typical of Zelazny's fully-drawn characters. He believes that form and chaos are reflected in all of us and that this is the basis for the human condition.

The imagery of the story superbly supports both its main theme, fertility, and its main symbol, the rose. The fertility theme is underscored by three major images. The first of these is implied by the reference to William Blake's poem "The Sick Rose." The general sexual nature of the poem is well-known, and the specific image of the worm penetrating the flower in that poem without question mimics the sexual act itself. The allusion to the poem thus emphasizes fertility in its sexual sense.

The second major image is found in Gallinger's reference to the Devadais of India as he watches Braxa dance the first time. These street dancers, he reflects, spin their colorful webs and draw in the male insect. The image specifically recalls two instances in nature where the female uses sex to net the male. First is the female black widow spider who draws the male into her web to mate by spinning a very specific pattern and then kills him when the act is complete. Like her, Braxa spins a web of dance, mates with Gallinger, and then figuratively kills him. Second is the pheromonic behavior of many insects. In these instances, the female secretes a chemical which acts as a sexual attractant.

The third major image is that of Mars "like a swollen belly" in the last sentence of the story. Certainly, this implies pregnancy and suggests that the whole planet is about to burst forth with new life.

Several other images in the story take on sexual connotations when considered within the broader fertility patterns. One such example is found in the image of a "colorful flag on a high pole," which is mentioned in conjunction with Gallinger's comment about Havelock Ellis' area of greatest popularity—sex. It suggests erection. Another is found in the net images which are scattered throughout the story. They suggest Gallinger being drawn into the love affair, both sexually and emotionally. Another is found in "belly-stung buffalo," which would swell as a woman's stomach would in pregnancy, and yet another is found in Gallinger's description of his Martian dictionary growing daily like a tulip that will soon bloom.

"A Rose for Ecclesiastes" is one of Zelazny's best stories. It is well-conceived and well-executed. Already recognized as a science fiction classic, its portrayal of a genuinely human character betrayed by his own arrogance and its exploration of the fertility theme raise it to the level of literature.

1. Thomas F. Monteleone, "Fire and Ice—On Roger Zelazny's Short Fiction," *Algol*, 13, No. 2 (Summer 1976), 10.
2. Martin Nurmi, *William Blake* (Kent, OH: Kent State University Press, 1976), p. 68.
3. H. F. Peters, *Ranier Maria Rilke: Masks and the Man* (Seattle, WA: University of Washington Press, 1960), p. 183.
4. Peters, p. 165.
5. Ibid., p. 160.
6. Ibid., p. 171.
7. Ibid., p. 169.
8. Havelock Ellis, *The Dance of Life* (London: Constable and Company, 1923), pp. x-xi.

IV.

THIS IMMORTAL

Despite its title, Zelazny's Hugo award winning novel, *This Immortal*, is not ultimately about immortality. Rather, the broader theme of the book is renewal or restoration. In terms of the ever-present form and chaos philosophy, it deals with the re-forming process which follows destruction. Specifically, it treats the problem of preserving and restoring an Earth which has been almost totally devastated in a nuclear holocaust. This post-bomb setting is a familiar one to Zelazny readers.

That Zelazny is not focusing on immortality is reflected in the handling of the title. The story first appeared as " . . . And Call Me Conrad" in the October and November, 1965, issues of the *Magazine of Fantasy and Science Fiction* and won the Hugo in 1966 for the best novel under that title. *This Immortal* was selected by Ace Books, because, at the time, they preferred titles that were short and simple. (1)

The story is set on Earth at an undetermined time long after the "Three Days," an atomic war which while it did not completely destroy all life, did reduce civilization to survival level. At the time of the story, Earth is an island civilization. Its ruined cities are inhabited by various plant, animal, and human mutations, and its continents are still too radioactive to sustain any normal life. The radiation and the mutated forms make it both a hostile and dangerous place.

The main body of Earth's surviving population had long ago left it to establish colonies on Mars and Titan. Then, after a century of self-sufficiency, an inter-stellar vehicle was developed which brought the colonists into contact with the Vegans, a superior and alien life-form. This permitted the colonists to spread to Taler, Bekab, and "a couple dozen other worlds in the Vegan combine."

Four million people still live on Earth, which is run by the Earthgov on the planet Taler as a curiosity for the Vegans who had never encountered a totally ruined planet before. Earth is treated as if it were an enormous museum, complete with tours for visiting Vegans. Preservation of historical sites, as well as their restoration, and tourism are under the direction of the Commissioner of Arts, Monuments, and Archives. He is Conrad Nomikos, the novel's main character.

The Vegans are generally hated by the Earthmen. At the least, they are viewed with suspicion. The reasons for this are many, but primarily the Earthmen feel that they are being exploited, that their world has been turned into a brothel, and that the Vegans think of them as provincial. There is a great deal of truth in all these reasons.

Politically, the resentment of the Vegans had generated a revolutionary group known as Radpol nearly a century before the onset of the story. In turn, it had founded a Returnist movement to get Earth expatriates to come back home. The movement proved to be a dismal failure.

Conrad had founded the party and was also its organizer and leader, but under the identity of Karaghiosis. The Tom Paine of the movement was Phil Graber, now an aged poet. Both men came eventually to realize that the movement would fail and took actions to disengage themselves from it. Half a century before, Phil began to deny his associations with Radpol, and Conrad/Karaghiosis arranged a convenient death by having his big blazeboat break up in the bay at Pireaus. Even with the loss of its leader and founder, the movement did not die. Instead, it developed into a viable and effective counterforce.

The immediate conflict in the story is generated by the appearance of a Vegan named Cort Myshtigo, presumably present to write a travel book about Earth. He is the grandson of Tatram Yshtigo, an eminent philosopher, writer, and public administrator, and a man of great influence on Vega. To write his book, Cort has decided that he must make a tour of some of Earth's most important historic sites and that only Conrad will do for his guide.

Radpol believes that Cort's real mission is to survey Earth so that choice sites may be sold off to Vegan developers. Radpol's representatives are a volcanic Latin named Dos Santos and a tall, slim, and lovely girl named Diane. She wears a red wig to cover an ugly scar that she received from a Vegan disease that she contracted in her youth while working as a pleasure girl at one of the resorts. Both believe that Cort's visit will mean the end of their hopes for a regenerated Earth and have decided that he must die. To carry out the assassination, they have hired an Arab named Hassan, the world's last living mercenary and one of its foremost hired killers.

As with "A Rose for Ecclesiastes," the primary theme of *This Immortal* is fertility, or restoration in a broader sense. We are made aware of it in two ways. First, the plot action itself develops out of a concern for the preservation and re-population of Earth. This is the motive for Radpol's actions. It is also Conrad's motive, except that he believes that the Returnist movement is dead and that re-population by virtue of the colonists returning home is not possible. As the story eventually unfolds, it is also Cort's motive for being on Earth. Second, the characterization of Conrad supports the fertility theme.

As with most of the heroes in Zelazny's work, Conrad is an extremely complex construction. He was designed to function at the physical level of the novel as well as at various symbolic levels.

Physically, he is Conrad Nomikos, Commissioner of Arts, Monuments, and Archives. He admits to being two-hundred and thirty-four years old and says that aging stopped between twenty and thirty. He is incredibly strong and well over six feet tall. His left cheek is purpled from a mutant fungus he picked up while disinterring the Guggenheim Museum for a New York tour. He has mis-matched eyes (one is cold-blue, the other is brown), a short right leg which requires that he wear a build-up boot, a hairline that peaks within a fingerbreadth of his brow, and an extrasensory ability called "pseudopathic wish fulfillment" that permits him to see and hear people without actually being in their presence. Unfortunately, he can neither control its use nor call it up at will. He is a mutant himself and may be immortal. Whether or not the condition is permanent, he does not know.

Psychologically, he is in the mold of many other Zelazny heroes. He is hard on the outside, extremely capable of doing what he feels must be done, but sensitive and understanding on the inside. Like Hell Tanner, he is a rebel, very individualistic, very active, very confident. He has a peculiarly romantic perspective and the soul of a poet. He is capable of deep love and is attracted to beautiful women. He trusts his instincts and his intuition.

As is often the case with his early writing, Zelazny links Conrad to several mythologic and historic characters by allusion. The clustering of these identities about the central core that is Conrad tends to strengthen those qualities which are common to all and opens up broad possibilities in terms of symbolic significance. Either directly or indirectly, Conrad is linked to Hephaestus, the Emperor Constantine, Karaghiosis, Lord Hades, Papa Legba, Dionysius, and others. From these identities, three principal characteristics emerge: caretaker of the underworld, fertility figure, and instrument of change.

Moreover, it is obvious that some of the events of the novel itself are either taken directly from or suggested by the legends, myths, or stories connected with these identities.

Though the scope of this study does not permit an elaboration of how each identity amplifies that of Conrad, two examples will establish how the characterization process works.

The Greek god Hephaestus, or Vulcan as he is known to the Romans, is never mentioned by name in *This Immortal*, but he is introduced into the story early by means of the ballad of the limping boy who breaks the back of Themocles after wrestling with him for three days. Close examination of the myths surrounding Hephaestus and Vulcan reveal that they form the basis for the physical description of Conrad. Both the god and Conrad are described as lame, ugly, and incredibly strong. Both were rejected by their parents because of their deformities and left out in the elements as children to die.

There are also other parallels between the two. Both are destined to overthrow their superiors. Hephaestus is destined to overthrow Zeus in one legend, and Conrad, as Karaghiosis, tried to overthrow the Vegans through Radpol. Both bear a patronistic relationship to art and culture. Hephaestus is known as the patron of artisans and he is the God of Fire, fire as it is associated with "the forge, the creative flame." (2) As Commissioner of Arts, Monuments, and Archives, Conrad is the person most responsible for preserving and restoring the art and culture of Earth. Also, both the god and Conrad are associated with the underworld. Because of his association with flame, Hephaestus raises the image of flame, and flame is, of course, hell's most identifiable quality. On the other hand, Conrad inherits a devastated Earth, whose predominant feature is radioactivity, another kind of fire. Metaphorically, Earth is the underworld.

Another example of how the characterization process works is found in the character of Karaghiosis. It is the name under which Conrad founded Radpol and carried out its revolutionary activities, but it is also the name of the central figure in Greek and Turkish "shadow drama." Created by throwing the shadow of a pasteboard puppet against a white linen curtain, Karaghiosis is best known and most loved of the shadow play characters. He is played as comic, ribald, cunning, and bellicose. Paul McPharlin describes him as follows:

> He has been compared with Punch, though they have only the slapstick in common. Often accompanied by an obtuse crony who serves as a feeder for his jokes, Karaghiosis makes himself at home in any sort of play, interrupting even the romantic and serious with his sallies. Playing for an all-male audience, he is outspoken about his sexual exploits; his Turkish progenitor wore a huge phallus in the manner of the players in ancient Greek farce. (3)

The shadow-play Karaghiosis reinforces two of Conrad's major personality characteristics. The fertility parallel is obvious, but equally important is the association that the reader is apt to make with the underworld because of the "shadow" nature of the character. The Greeks pictured the underworld as a "dark and gloomy place" and "the counterpart to that of Zeus, a dim, shadowy copy of life on earth. All the awfulness of death gathered about the king and queen of the shades. . . . " (4) By virtue of his unsurpassed popularity, Karaghiosis is the foremost figure of the shadow world and therefore comparable to Conrad who is keeper of Earth, metaphorically the underworld in *This Immortal.*

Without going into great detail, it is important to mention certain aspects of the relationship between Conrad and Dionysius. First, both figures reflect the form and chaos philosophy. Edith Hamilton says that Dionysius was both man's benefactor and his destroyer, and in that capacity he mimicked the wine which he represented. While it brought great benefit to man and symbolized fertility, it often caused him to commit frightful and atrocious crimes. (5) More importantly, he is part of the model for the "dying and reviving gods," first mentioned in Frazer's *Golden Bough* and later picked up in Jessie L. Weston's *From Ritual to Romance.* (6) Conrad also fits this model, which is a common one in Zelazny's early writing.

Before dealing with that aspect of Conrad's characterization, however, it is necessary to mention another parallel which exists. It is between Conrad and the Prometheus of Shelley's poem, "Prometheus Unbound." There are several interesting points of comparison between the two, and it is likely that Shelley's Prometheus was primarily responsible for shaping Conrad. The poem is introduced into the novel by Phil Graber. It is important at the action level of the book because it is on the blank pages at the back of his copy that Phil writes his reasons as to why Cort Myshtigo must live and explains that Tatram had found a way to preserve Earth's cultural integrity and to return it to autonomy.

33

The parallels between Conrad and Prometheus follow. First, Prometheus gives fire to man. It is the fire of creativity from which civilizations are made. (7) Conrad, too, brings the promise of renewal to Earth. Because he inherits it, he holds the possibility for recreating civilization in the palm of his hand, and by virtue of his role as "dying and reviving god," he guarantees that Earth will be restored.

Both characters are supported by "Mother Earth." In Conrad's case, Earth has made him virtually immortal. Both are sustained by thoughts of their brides: Prometheus by Asia and Conrad by Cassandra. Both are chained to rocks in the course of their adventures. For Prometheus, this act is a symbol of despotism, a restraint upon man's intellectual fulfillment and spiritual freedom. For Conrad, it is a symbol of the thinking which produced the "Three Days." Conrad's ultimate goals are the same as those of Prometheus, to fill his life with experience in an environment which is free. Both characters are freed when they renounce hatred and revenge and accept love. Though the specific circumstances differ in each case, the pattern of their emotional development is similar. Conrad's unwillingness to kill Cort himself and, further, to let Radpol kill him shows that he has progressed far beyond the hatred and revenge which caused him to create Radpol in the first place and to lead its revolutionary bombings and assassinations. His deep feeling for Cassandra shows that he has reached a maturity which permits psychologically healthy love.

There is one final and important comparison. In his "Preface" to *Prometheus Unbound*, Shelley compares his main character to that of Satan in Milton's *Paradise Lost*. Shelley's point is that though Prometheus and Satan are very similar characters—both exhibit courage, majesty, and firm and patient opposition to omnipotent force—their motives are different. Prometheus's motives are pure and true, but Satan's are tainted by ambition, envy, and revenge.

The comparison is an interesting one, for it is clear that Zelazny intends for his readers to visualize Conrad as a "Satanic" figure. Several clues indicate this. One of Conrad's names is Kallikanzaros, the Greek word for devil. Also, Conrad is associated with the "horny ones" as they are referred to in the novel, and there is a connection between Hassan's respect for *shaitan*, or devil, and his respect for Conrad.

It is clear that Zelazny wishes us to view the "devil" as a sympathetic figure. We are not to think of him as the evil Satan of Christianity, but rather as one of the well-respected lords of the underworld, like Lord Hades, or one of the *shaitans*, who are distinguished in Arabic lore as a class of jinn. That we are meant to interpret Conrad this way is supported by his continuous association with various mythological caretakers of the underworld.

There is no question but that Zelazny intends Conrad to be his own variation of the mythical "dying and reviving gods." The key to this interpretation is to be found in the concept of heroes as it evolves in the novel. Heroes are important to the working out of the Earth's problems, and Conrad fills the hero concept, even though he spends a great deal of time denying it.

Redwig introduces the idea in a conversation she has with Conrad about Phil Graber's philosophy: "The age of strange beasts is come upon us again. Also, the age of heroes, demigods" (TI, p. 98), she says. Moreover, though Phil is demeaned throughout the story as a half-talent, he proves in the end to be correct and alters the course of Conrad's actions. So, he achieves credibility despite Conrad making light of the hero idea.

Conrad is regarded as a hero under his identity as Karaghiosis, and his subsequent success in overthrowing Vegan control of Earth, regardless of the means, establishes him as a hero under his identity as Conrad. The sheer weight of his success places him in the hero-demigod category. Moreover, he fits the definition of a hero as it is laid out by Thomas Carlyle, despite the fact that there is a scene in the novel mocking hero-worship and that he calls Carlyle a fool. Conrad fits the definition because he displays an extraordinary consciousness of the master plan for the world and because the history of Earth as it will become will be the history of Conrad himself. This aligns perfectly with Carlyle's statement that " . . . the history of what man has accomplished in the world, is at bottom the History of the Great Men who have worked here." (9)

The facts of *This Immortal* clearly belie Conrad's denial of the hero concept, regardless of how hard he protests. It is his existence and immortality which permit the resolution of Earth's problem. Moreover, it is his instinct for keeping Cort alive and his actions to that effect that create the conditions for restoration of the planet.

Further evidence is found in Conrad's purpose in the novel, which is exclusively to restore Earth's former fertility. This places him squarely in the mold of the grail-quest heroes identified by Jessie L. Weston. After analyzing several variations of the grail myth, she states that " . . . the land becomes Waste, and the task of the hero is that of restoration." (10) She concludes that the heroes are themselves variations of Sir James G. Frazer's "dying and reviving gods."

Once again invoking the Frazer model, Zelazny adapts several elements. His modifications are made, of course, to fit the needs of his story. His handling of the death and revival part of the model is one example. Because of the limitations he has imposed in the world of the novel, he cannot justify Conrad's literal death. So, he does the next best thing. He has the identity of Karaghiosis die in the explosion of the blazeboat, and Conrad Nomikos appears. Figuratively, the god has died and been reborn.

Another element of the model is that the god is usually ripped or torn apart and the pieces of the body scattered. The feigned death of Karaghiosis mimes both the violent end and the scattering of the pieces.

Also, a flower or fruit often springs from the blood of the slain god. For example, pomegranates spring from the blood of Dionysius, anemones from the blood of Adonis, and violets from the blood of Attis. Zelazny alters this concept somewhat in his creation of the *strige-fleur*, which means vampire flower and which drinks blood. The connection between blood and flower is maintained but once again modified to suit the needs of the novel. .

35

There is also the inevitable relationship between the dead god and the underworld. It was logical to assume that when the vegetation disappeared its anthropomorphic equivalent had gone underground. It was also logical to assume, by extension and recurrence, that the god was Lord of the Underworld. Such a connection exists with Tammuz, Adonis, Hyacinth, Dionysius, and Osiris. It is easy to understand, then, why Zelazny has taken such care to connect Conrad with various underworld caretakers, since Earth more closely resembles Hell than any place else.

There are other elements of the model carried out in both Conrad and the story itself. Conrad plays the syrinx for the satyrs, for example, and both Attis and Marsyas were known as pipers, while the death of Adonis was annually mourned to the shrill, wailing notes of the flute. Moreover, both the island of Kos and the month of October are connected to the model. It is no accident that Zelazny makes Conrad's sanctuary the island of Kos and begins the story in October.

Other connections with the model are found in the restoration of fertility to the land and the healing of the wounded king. That Conrad will restore Earth's fertility is borne out by the remarks he makes near the end of the novel about repopulation and cleaning up the Earth. Moreover, Weston found in her examination of the various grail-myths that the restoration of the land is connected directly to healing of a wounded king, (11) and curiously Earth's fertility is restored after Conrad's mutant fungus is destroyed by the irradiated rock.

In his construction of Conrad, Zelazny chose to make him both hero and wounded king. This is not a common combination in the grail-legends, but it does also occur there, and it is far more efficient for the needs of *This Immortal.*

Even though immortality is not the primary theme of the novel, it is critical to the story's development. Without it, Earth's restoration could not occur, for no one but Conrad, or someone equally as long-lived, would be around to oversee it.

Immortality is an abiding Zelazny theme and one that he is interested in exploring for its own sake. Cort asks the author's own question at the beginning of *This Immortal* when he says, " . . . I was curious as to what sensibilities a human might cultivate, given so much time . . . " (TI, pp. 22-23). In the development of Conrad through the course of the novel, Zelazny answers his own question.

What we learn of immortality, however, reaches far deeper than a mere summation of Conrad's attitudes and actions, for he is not a particularly good judge of his own development despite his age. On the surface, he appears pessimistic and cynical, denying idealism and heroism. But there is a contradiction in his makeup that betrays a deeper, positive attitude and exposes his cynicism and pessimism as a mask. This shows most clearly in his attitude towards instinct and intuition. Though he constantly denies the validity of Cassandra's instincts, he falls back upon his own time and again when he is placed under pressure. It is instinct, for example, which makes him keep Cort alive.

His surface attitudes are those born from living a long time, from watching men try hard to prove that they are fools. He expresses this most clearly when he says that Phil Graber had lived too long because it had given him the opportunity to write a lot of bad poetry. Conrad, himself, has passed beyond the spontaneous energy of youth, beyond the capacity to be inflamed by ideals and causes. He has become more worldly, more wise, more realistic. His attitudes are easier to understand when he is viewed in his symbolic role of "dying and reviving god." He is a sympathetic reflection of the Earth itself, jaded and worn, and curiously ruined. Cort establishes the connection in a comment he makes about how Conrad is almost like the spirit of the Earth (TI, p. 22). Like it, he will endure. Like it, he will be renewed.

Conrad's own renewal has already begun when the story starts. It began with his relationship to Cassandra, a nymphish girl of twenty, graceful, tall, beautiful, and web-fingered. He recalls that when he first saw her she was "sunning herself like a mermaid." The web-fingers and mermaid references clearly establish her relationship to the sea, and the sea, in the "dying and reviving god" model, is a symbol of renewal. Weston comments that a ceremonial marriage very frequently formed a part of the "Fertility Ritual" and was supposed to be especially helpful in the "freeing of the waters" so that restoration of the land could take place. (12) And, indeed, Frazer cites several instances where water plays a significant part in the restoration process.

Cassandra's role is reinforced when like Ishtar, in one of the common fertility myths, she disappears for a time, only to return later to rescue Conrad. During this time, she is believed to be dead, swallowed up by an earthquake. So, symbolically, she parallels Ishtar's annual trip to the underworld. Her return not only saves Conrad's life, but floods him with new emotion as well, thus paralleling Ishtar's restoration of fertility to the land.

Zelazny's comments on immortality are, in the long run, rather simple. He believes that longevity should provide a person the opportunity to fill his life with experiences so that he will continue to grow. Experience is its own excuse for being, and certainly, Zelazny would agree that the present life-span is far too short to permit man to develop all of his potential, especially his mental abilities. Beyond that, he feels that an individual should develop style and that long life permits that.

Once again, the form and chaos philosophy is reflected in the story. The "dying and reviving god" model reflects it, and the novel itself is a broad metaphor for it. This is shown in the state of civilization as it is reported in the story. Prior to the "Three Days," it was highly technical, very well-developed. After the "Three Days," there was a period of chaos, which is being overtaken by a second period of form when the story ends.

As usual, those same forces are displayed in the character Conrad himself. This is objectively illustrated in his physical appearance. Redwig describes him, " 'You have two profiles. From the right side you are a demigod; from the left you are a demon' " (TI, p. 183). Form and chaos

37

are also reflected in his actions. First the destroyer and assassin, he becomes the reformer.

This is the human condition as Zelazny sees it. Man's intellect is constantly at war with his emotion, his will with his desire, his ideals with his environment. This friction produces guilt which means that he will never be wholly right or wrong in his acts. These dichotomies are part of man's makeup, and they make him infinitely human.

Though *This Immortal* has been criticized as uncertain in plot, which it is, and the character of Conrad has been faulted for being too unsympathetic to the world about him, (13) which is a matter of judgment, it is a great first effort. Feeling his way along in his first novel-length story, Zelazny's most notable fault may simply be not exerting tight enough control over those characters he has created. Or, it may simply be that adding material to " . . . And Call Me Conrad" to bring it up to book length prevented him from bringing his own sense of form fully to bear on the material. Regardless, *This Immortal* will continue to exert its own charms over its readers, for it does create a sense of wonder.

1. Roger Zelazny, "Unpublished Letter," June 23, 1977.
2. Pierre Grimal, ed., *Larousse World Mythology* (London: The Hamlyn Publishing Group, 1969), p. 129.
3. Paul McPharlin, *The Puppet Theater in America, A History 1524-1948* (Boston: Plays Incorporated, 1969), p. 290.
4. Arthur Fairbanks, *A Handbook of Greek Religion* (New York: American Book Company, 1910), p. 184.
5. Edith Hamilton, *Mythology* (Boston: The New American Library, 1942), p. 60.
6. Ibid., pp. 61-62.
7. Fairbanks, p. 163.
8. Thomas Hutchinson, ed., *Shelley: Poetical Works* (London: Oxford University Press, 1967), p. 205.
9. Thomas Carlyle, *On Heroes and Hero Worship* (New York: Dutton, 1964), p. 239.
10. Jessie L. Weston, *From Ritual to Romance* (Garden City, NJ: Doubleday Anchor Books, 1957), p. 23.
11. Ibid., p. 48.
12. Weston, p. 31.
13. Joseph Sanders, "Zelazny: Unfinished Business," in *Voices for the Future*, ed. Thomas D. Clareson (Bowling Green, OH: Bowling Green University Popular Press, 1978), II, 15.

V.

THE DOORS OF HIS FACE, THE LAMPS OF HIS MOUTH

1965, 1966, and 1967 were banner years for Zelazny. During that period, he not only won a Hugo and two Nebula awards, but he received at least nine other nominations for these major science fiction prizes. One of the stories from this period, "The Doors of His Face, the Lamps of His Mouth," won a Nebula and received a Hugo nomination, attesting both to its popularity and its quality. More than a decade later, it remains one of Zelazny's very best pieces of writing and provides an excellent example of how he worked at the time.

In his "Introduction" to *Four for Tomorrow*, Theodore Sturgeon expressed exasperation at Zelazny's use of "exotic references," "absolutely precise and therefore untranslatable German philosophic terms," and mythological citations. (1) And though Sturgeon's criticism is justified, it fails to recognize the purpose behind these characteristics of Zelazny's early style.

To explain them, it is first necessary to come to a more complete understanding of Zelazny's views of learning and his own writing process at this point in his career. These are best expressed in his own words.

> I once mentioned in passing something that I called a Da Vinci syndrome, when speaking about educational theory. I believe that knowledge can hit a critical mass. I think that one's total body of knowledge—if one consciously directs its acquisition toward the building up of a full-spectrum world picture—will come to function almost autonomously as an approximation of the world itself [in other words, as a metaphor] so that the addition of any new material is no longer a simple additive process, but rather, will result in an exponential increase in the total that one possesses [that is, a kind of metamorphic process]. It is not just a question of learning or not learning lots of stuff initially, but in deciding what should be learned and how much of it, in order to reach a critical mass as soon as possible, so that future learning, even if desultory-sounding to an outsider, will result in a great number of things being learned from the digestion of a single fact, rather than simply the fact itself. (2)

The writing process itself, he compares to a tennis stroke.

> ... each motion/position/pressure/etc. of hand/wrist/arm/etc. required individual attention while the entire act was being learned; yet the total movement must take only an instant when playing the game. In other words, in writing as well as learned physical activity you intentionally transform a greater number of separate items into a single reflex so that you can do it without thinking much about the process itself, keeping your mind free for overall strategy. Initially, one does this mainly with the mechanical aspects

of writing, the sheer business of keeping the prose interesting and grammatically sound. Continuing from there, I think that, ideally, the more you write the more things you come to entrust to the unconscious at its reflex level. If you go in for a good number of metaphors, say, it seems that the unconscious begins providing them almost unsolicited after a time. If you have worked hard at constructing good metaphors for a very long time, the process does seem to sink in to the point where those which arise unbidden eventually become quite appropriate—often in ways which are not always immediately obvious. This is a kind of breakthrough, as I see it. The reflex has been extended to the point where you have begun tapping deeper levels of your mind rather than just flexing surface ingenuity, down there where your whole world picture is stored. If this is correct, and it feels correct, then you cannot help but bring to bear everything in your mind that resonates with whatever you are doing at that moment—without giving it as much directed attention as will seem to have gone into the piece. If the result is then taken apart by a perceptive reader, he will often spot elaborate constructions and contrivances; things which are really there, but things which sometimes prompt questions such as, "How could he be thinking of this, that, and the other thing all at once?" The answer, of course, is that it was not a product of directed attention. There is not world enough or time to run it all through the mind in linear fashion. We cheat time by chopping up, say, a thousand hours' worth of thinking into a thousand one-hour segments and running them all through the mind in an hour with each of a thousand reflexes with its particular allotment simultaneously. So you translate your thinking into words and to the reader it is one apparent quick movement, like a tennis stroke. It is the work which went into developing the stroke which is the key to the paradox of the simple movement's containing masses of complexities. You have to multiply it by the thousand other instants which accompanied it through the writer's mind. (3)

Once having digested these passages, two questions must logically follow. First, how do they relate to one another? Second, how do they apply to any individual story?

The answer to the first is that the "tennis stroke" process automatically monitors both the writer's conscious and subconscious minds on several tracks simultaneously and selects material for him to use in his story which reflects his full-spectrum world picture.

In a growing person, the world picture would be ever-changing. Each new bit of information processed into it would cause some modification of it, as T. S. Eliot explains in "Tradition and the Individual Talent." Usually, such information would produce a refinement, the unifying of loose ends, or an affirmation of values, but a highly traumatic experience might produce considerable reshaping.

The answer to the second question is a matter of logic. Any individual story is the product of the total, internalized world picture but also is focused in such a way as to reflect some particular aspect of it. In other words, it becomes a touchstone between author and reader which facilitates the communication of the chosen value. It creates a vehicle through which the reader may explore his own world picture. Obviously, the better the writer has created the vehicle, the more perfect the communication between himself and his reader. Generalized, it also permits the reader to explore man.

If written well enough, the story will permit the reader to experience many of those unconscious elements which the author has drawn into his material, many of which he is, himself, unaware.

From another point of view, the whole of the story becomes an extended metaphor promoting the exchange of experience.between author and reader, an interface. Perhaps this is best stated by Robert Heilman, however, in his brilliant study of *King Lear*. On the function of metaphor, he writes:

> . . . the sole point is that a series of dramatic statements about one subject does constitute a bloc of meaning which is a structural part of the play. This bloc may be understood as one of the author's metaphors. It is a metaphor just as a body of recurrent images, with its burden of implications, is a metaphor. The dramatist's basic metaphor is his plot. All of his metaphors are valid parts of his total meaning, the search for which must include a study of the relationships among the parts. All of the constituent metaphors must be related to the large metaphor which is the play itself. (4)

The extended metaphor becomes a vehicle for the reader to get outside of himself and to extend himself beyond the bounds of his own experience. By incorporating various allusions and dramatic actions which explore the same conceptual and experiential territory into his story, the author creates a community of meaning. By repetition, these communities of meaning become symbols which permit statements about the "larger meaning" of the work. When all the elements of the story, its actions, characters, properties, themes, and symbols create a close functional coalescence, then, the work itself becomes an organism. (5) The result of this integration of meaning into metaphoric patterns is to create multiple avenues for the reader to explore and to give the stories, themselves, an open-ended quality.

This is the method of Zelazny's stories. The exotic references, the philosophic terms, and the classic citations are not objects extraneous to the story. On the contrary, they are intricate to the development of its metaphoric patterns, and they are the touchstones for the extraction of the meaning of the "larger metaphor" of the story, bearing in mind all the while that it is itself but a metaphor for the writer's internalized world picture.

In the last analysis, "The Doors of His Face, the Lamps of His Mouth" is a story about maturation, about how experience can change a personality, about how for some it is necessary to go through a traumatic situation to continue to grow.

Like so many of Zelazny's stories, "Doors/Lamps" finds its basic substructure in religion. In this case, it is the Book of Job. Typically, however, the analogue provides a general background with several similarities rather than simply being translated into another form.

The first indication of the relationship between "Doors/Lamps" and Job is found in the title. "The Doors of His Face, the Lamps of His Mouth" is drawn from the following passages in Job:

> Who can open *the doors of his face?*
> his teeth are terrible round about.
> His scales are his pride,
> shut together as with a close seal.
> Out *of his mouth* go burning *lamps,*
> and sparks of fire leap out.
>
> (41:14-19; emphasis mine.)

Not only does Zelazny draw the title of his story from these passages (by placing the words underlined in line 18 into parallel construction with those of line 14), he also draws the general concept of the leviathan and the personality fault of pride for the characterization of Carlton Davits from it.

Since both "Doors" and Job are stories of maturation, or character metamorphosis, which focus on a single figure, it is reasonable to expect that we would find a number of similarities between them. This is the case.

Both Davits and Job suffer from the same major fault, extreme pride. Though neither displays arrogance, their pride is of such depth and strength that it blocks both of them from the insight that each needs to grow psychologically.

The similarities extend, however, much farther than just the basic character fault. For one thing, the pattern of their development is roughly similar. Both hold high status in their respective cultures, both fall from that state, both are subsequently tested, and both are left with visible physical damage as a result of that testing. Finally, both eventually achieve maturity. Of course, there are also significant differences between the two. These are important because they show how Zelazny has modified Job to suit the demands of his story. Each of these similarities and differences will be briefly summarized.

Job is described as a man who has thousands of sheep and camels, five hundred each of oxen and she-asses, and a very great household (1:3). Davits is the man who once owned Tensquare (an atomic-powered ship the size of a football field), is a playboy, and when he is divorced from Jean Luharich, Zelazny writes, "No alimony. Many $ on both sides . . . Young. Both. Strong. Rich and spoiled as hell. Ditto" (DF, p. 19).

Even though both protagonists are rich and powerful at the outset, however, there is a significant difference in what this has brought each of them in his personal relationships. Initially, Job has deep and meaningful relationships with family, friends, and God. Davits, on the other hand, has developed no such relationships. He has too much money and too little responsibility. He uses people. He does not understand that both love and friendship require giving as well as taking. The difference between the two is important, because in Davits' characterization, Zelazny is reflecting the view of our times—money and influence are more important than meaningful human relationships.

Both men fall from high states, but the cause in each instance is different. Job falls because God permits Satan to test him. The impetus for his fall is generated outside himself. Davits' fall, by contrast, is self-generated. It is the result of overplaying his hand, of being too sure, of failing to recognize that he could fail.

Both men are tested. Job must face those trials imposed upon him by Satan, while Davits must face those imposed by his own fear. Though the tests are different, the results are the same. Both lose material wealth, suffer losses in personal relationships, and sustain physical pain. Job receives "sore boils from the sole of his foot unto his crown" (2:7-8), while Davits is left with partial hemiplegia as a result of his first attempt to capture Ikky and later receives bad wounds from the screw of the *Dolphin* in a diving accident.

Though there are many similarities between Job and Davits and though there is little question that the character of Davits is drawn from that of Job, Zelazny has cast Davits as a contemporary figure, one with whom his audience can identify more readily. He is, in fact, a restless rebel more concerned with love of woman than of God, who is highly psychologized and personalized.

The parallels between "Doors" and Job do not end here. The general concept for Ikky comes from Chapter 41 of that book. Following is a composite of the Biblical leviathan pictured in Job. He is so fierce that no one dare stir him up, so overwhelming that a man is cast down even at his sight, so strong that iron is as straw and brass as rotten wood against him. His scales are welded together like armor, his teeth are "terrible round about," and a light shines by his "neesings" (nose holes: Job 41: 18). Fire burns from his mouth, his breath will kindle coals, smoke pours from his nostrils, and his eyes are like "the eyelids of the morning."

As impressive as this description is, it is not one which a contemporary reader can deal with easily. It is too subjective and remote. So, Zelazny makes it concrete by focusing the image and giving it an identifiable referent. Specifically, he combines Job's leviathan with the *plesiosaur*, a water reptile from the Mesozoic era thought to be extinct but often put forth as the Loch Ness Monster.

From Job, Zelazny retains the general impression of huge size, awesome strength, and heartstopping fearsomeness, but he focuses the image as follows. First, he gives Ikky definite dimension, a hundred meters or more. Then, he makes the terrible teeth into fangs and the eyelids of morning into round, lidless eyes like roulette wheels. He eliminates the scales except as articulations over the eyes, colors it green, and gives it a neck "like a giant beanstalk." He makes the head fat and craggy and indicates that Ikky is not very bright. Finally, he implies that it has some sort of flipper arrangement. Making Ikky more identifiable to his readers is important because the monster is a major symbol in the story, conveying

Carl's psychological problem through it.

Zelazny also draws the dominant field of imagery for "Doors" from Job. In the Biblical Book, water images symbolize the randomness of life, a fact which Job only comes to accept after he achieves maturity. In its capacity to be either creative or destructive, water illustrates the final relationship between Job and God.

In "Doors" the water pattern forms a dominant sub-metaphor which is so well integrated into the story that it serves multiple purposes. First, it functions at the literal level as the medium through which Davits must travel to catch an Ikky. Second, as rain, it marks the end of his vanity and the beginning of his maturity. (It marks the same transition for Jean Luharich.) Third, as the symbol of the sea, it functions at the psychological level as an equivalent to Davits' own mind and, at the mythological level, as an equivalent to hell.

Tied closely to the water pattern is the voyage motif. During the course of the story, Carl makes both physical and mental journeys. Physically, he travels across the seas of Venus and down into their depths. Psychologically, he travels deep into the recess of his own mind to confront his fear, symbolized by Ikky.

These variations of the water pattern are appropriate to the basic purpose of the story because they help to reinforce, focus, and define it.

Another important sub-metaphor is the sight-insight pattern. It also functions at multiple levels of the story: first, at the physical level of sight, or lack of it; and second, at the psychological level of insight, or once again, lack of it. This pattern is developed by many different devices and established almost at the outset of the story by the scene in which Carl describes his descent to Venus:

> When you break into *Cloud* Alley it [the continent of Hand] swings its silverblack bowling ball toward you without warning. . . . Next, you study Hand to lay its *illusion* and the two middle fingers become dozen-ringed archipelagoes as the outers *resolve* into green-gray peninsulas . . . (DF, p. 1—Emphasis mine).

In this brief scene, Zelazny sketches the psychological journey that Carl will make. Before his encounter with Ikky, his vision is clouded, his insight is blocked, he does not grow from his experience. Then, after being cast down by the sight of the monster, he goes through a period of illusion, where all he sees is through an alcoholic stupor. Finally, his mental and physical suffering begins to bear fruit and the distortion resolves to clear images. Each of the key words—"clouds," "illusion," and "resolve"—has a conceptual relationship to sight.

Other devices also support the sight-insight pattern. The scene cast as a movie scenario, for example, reflects Carl's general attitude at the time that the story begins. It is somewhat cynical and pessimistic, but he is on his way to a realistic view of himself and the world around him. The camera, in particular, has come to represent the masking of truth for him. This is reinforced by his many comments about cameras, cameramen, and Anderson, Jean's publicity man. Carl's general attitude is reinforced by the many instances of distorted vision in the story. Malvern's cabin, for example, is seen "through a glass, brownly" (DF, p. 12).

The most important device in the sight-insight pattern, however, is the symbol of eyes, especially as it relates to Jean. Before discussing it, though, it is necessary to more closely define the relationship between Carl and Jean.

Two key comments by Carl show that she is a psychological reflection of himself. The first is a response to Mike Dabis' suggestion that Jean might wish to re-establish her relationship with Carl (they had been married for three months several years earlier). He says, "No good, no good . . . We're both fission chambers by nature. You can't have jets on both ends of the rocket and expect to go anywhere—what's in the middle just gets smashed" (DF, p. 26). The second occurs when Jean hooks an Ikky but cannot push the inject button to kill it because she is paralyzed with fear from looking into the beast's eyes. She asks Carl to do it and he replies, "No. If I do, you'll wonder for the rest of your life whether you could have. You'll throw away your soul finding out. I know you will, because we're alike, and I did it that way" (DF, p. 32).

A closer examination of the personalities of Carl and Jean affirms their correspondence. Both were young, rich, strong, and spoiled. Both are also stubborn, highly competitive, very athletic, reckless, love a challenge, have little respect for conventional rules, are quite capable, believed at one time that they could do anything, and are vain. Jean is not only vain herself but is also the solar system's ultimate peddler of vanity through her Cosmetics Company.

There is little doubt that Zelazny has created psychological mirror images or that he has once again drawn on Job for the nucleus of their characterizations. They are meant to be the "children of pride" referred to in 41:34 of that Book. Since that verse clearly stipulates that the leviathan is king over all the "children of pride," then, it is obvious that neither of them will be able to catch an Ikky until he or she has first conquered the beast within—vanity.

Besides serving as a psychological mirror, Jean also fulfills two other important functions: she is Carl's love-object and she is his guide to maturity. She is not conscious of this latter function, however, and Carl has only a vague awareness of it until she falters on the Inject. It is only then that he is fully aware that what is happening to her is exactly what happened to him. By making her go through with the act of killing the Ikky, he sacrifices his own opportunity to be the first to catch one of the great beasts, but he assures that she will achieve psychological wholeness without suffering the trauma that he did.

Jean-as-guide is best illustrated in the race scene under Tensquare. Even though Carl does not understand it completely at the time, he senses that she is a reflection of himself a few years earlier. Because of her actions and attitudes, he achieves a perspective of himself, and though this perspective makes him angry, it begins to focus his own thinking. It is through her actions during the race that Jean forces Carl from a passive to an

45

active posture and from a negative to a positive attitude. Passivity has been a problem for him since his first encounter with Ikky. His physical paralysis at the time became psychological.

Jean's actions are significant because she is an initiator. She prods him into the race and leads him throughout it, stepping up the pace to force him along. Her reckless use of her rockets, which places her in danger of being torn apart by the raft's windmill screws, requires Carl to act to save her. From that experience, both of them learn something about action: that there is a correct time, place, and situation for each act, that the degree of each act is critical, and that there is even a time, place, and situation for passivity.

Moreover, Jean forces Carl from his primarily passive posture toward life. This begins his preparation to accomplish two very important objectives: his successful confrontation with Ikky and his reconciliation with Jean, who is not only his love-object, but also the symbol of his love of self.

The race teaches Jean much the same lesson, except that she learns that some passivity is a virtue. It is the beginning of her own maturational process. Her realization of her own fallibility starts her toward a realistic perception of self and helps her to understand what Carl has gone through. Eventually, she will go through the same character metamorphosis that he does without the prolonged period of self-doubt and passivity.

Three acts performed by Jean just prior to the start of their race signal that she has begun her metamorphosis. First, she removes her violet contact lenses. This act, the removal of the primary symbol of her vanity, marks the clearing of her vision and the destruction of the barrier to mature insight. Second, she stops Anderson from taking publicity pictures of the race, which shows that she is sympathetic to Carl's perception of cameras. Third, when she recalls her own saving of Carl at Govino, tears flash into her eyes. This symbolizes a purgation, a freeing of the waters.

Besides the action pattern, there are also light-dark and descent patterns to reinforce the sight-insight complex. The light-dark pattern is especially appropriate because of the physical effect of light on sight and its figurative connection with insight. Even though Zelazny is limited to some degree in the use of light and dark images by the laws of physics, he maximizes its possibilities by careful planning of scene and time.

In general, Venus is painted as a planet of mist and sea and cloud, which is not only appropriate to Carl's mental state, but which also minimizes light. Several references establish it as a gray-to-dark world. Moreover, many of the story's scenes are set either at night or in storms, which further minimizes light. Extending the light-dark pattern is the descent pattern. Light diminishes with depth, so there is a natural connection.

To understand the significance of these supporting patterns, it is first necessary to discuss the meaning of two primary symbols of the story: the sea and Ikky. Psychologically, the sea represents Davits' mind and Ikky, the manifestation of his neurosis. For Carl to overcome his fear and to return to a healthy mental state, he must confront and defeat

46

it by destroying the leviathan which represents it. The descents that he makes into the sea, therefore, are symbolic descents into the dark areas of his own mind. Each time he descends, of course, he is moving from light to dark.

Three of Carl's descents are psychologically significant. The first is the race under Tensquare with Jean. Though it has already been discussed, it is important to note that it begins his preparation for a metamorphic change of personality by establishing Jean as his psychological guide and by precipitating a chain of events which restores his self-confidence. Moreover, it marks a change in their relationship. Prior to the race, each is locked into a rather traditional pattern of responses which is expected of divorced parties. His saving of her life changes that.

The second descent occurs on the "thirteenth day." It too is preparatory. Jean's long overcast of the line forces Carl to dive much deeper than he ever had before (she continues to drive him to a confrontation with his fear), and though he is terrified, he gets a grip on himself and carries out his duties. His remarks indicate that he is consciously aware of his problem, and when he finally reaches the deck of the raft safely, he laughs at his new-found confidence. He feels positive about his successful probe of his fear. The "thirteenth day" descent is important too, because when it is over, Jean apologizes to him for the overcast, displaying a genuine concern for his safety. Her admission of fallibility is yet another step towards their reconciliation.

The third descent, and most significant one, occurs on "the day of the beast." It brings Carl face to face with his fear. Psychologically, only his confrontation with his neurosis and his mastery of it will bring him mental health, and that, in turn, depends on his readiness. Carl is prepared and thus succeeds. His remark immediately prior to the confrontation with Ikky and his comparison to a bright comet indicate this. Zelazny means for us to see him as the comet: a body locked on course and speeding towards its destiny.

The light-dark pattern underscores his mental journey during the scene, and Ikky is tied into the dark side of it. Carl remarks, "I had finished attaching the leads and pulled the first plug when a big, rugged, *black* island drew beneath me. . . . " and "A giant *shadow* and a shock wave." (DF, p. 28—Emphasis added). By connecting Ikky to the dark imagery, Zelazny establishes him as a nightmare creature of the mind.

The contact between diver and beast recreates the conditions that originally triggered Carl's neurosis. His failure to act the first time shattered his self-confidence, plunged him into doubt and bankruptcy, and lead to the death of six men. This time it is different. He performs the only act that will save him. He pulls the plug on the squiggler and it immediately phosphoresces.

Once Carl performs his act of self-survival, the symbolic values for the light and dark clusters of images shift. This is as it should be because for the first time since his initial confrontation with Ikky, the conscious and subconscious elements of his mind have returned to their natural state of balance.

In accordance with Jungian psychodynamics, the period of Carl's neurosis is marked by the trapping of large quantities of psychic energy in the subconscious. This energy feeds that element which Jung calls "the shadow" and which is represented in the story by Ikky. (The enormous size of the beast is therefore a measure of the degree of Carl's neurosis.) When Carl pulls the plug on the squiggler, he releases the trapped energy and changes the nature of the subconscious itself. Whereas it was once a place filled with terror, it has now become a place of meditation, retreat, healing. That he blacks out after his panicked swim for the surface is both physically and psychologically appropriate.

That Carl has achieved a new psychological state is shown in the comments he makes as he is awaking, which constitute a short reiteration of man's evolution: "A few million years. I remember starting out as a one-celled organism, and painfully becoming an amphibian, then an air-breather. From somewhere high in the treetops, I heard a voice . . . I evolved into homosapience, then a step further into a hangover" (DF, p. 28). Because he has brought harmony to his psyche, he is quite literally a new man.

Jean also achieves maturity and a new and healthy relationship is created between them. For Zelazny, such a relationship is one which is in balance, which is creative, and which preserves the integrity of each party while promoting the growth of each. The Saturn symbol in the last line of the story perfectly emphasizes this union. Zelazny writes, " . . . but the rings of Saturn sing epithalamium the sea-beast's dower" (DF, p. 32).

The image is perfect. The bright planet glowing in the inky blackness of space visually suggests balance and the reconciliation of light and dark. All the antithetical elements of the story have been brought into a state of harmony. Moreover, the rings of Saturn themselves suggest union, completeness, and integrity, while being specifically connected to marriage. That they sing epithalamium echoes Kepler's "harmony of the spheres" and quite literally their dowry from the sea-beast is their perfect relationship.

There are three major allusions in "Doors," all of which add to the development of the story in significant ways. The first is to John Keats' poem "La Belle Dame Sans Merci." It occurs early in the novelette. Davits is sitting in Malvern's cabin thinking about his relationship with Jean and his fear of Ikky when he says, "I finished my drink and emptied my pipe. It was late and no songbirds were singing" (DF, p. 14). It is clearly a paraphrase of Keats' line "No birds sing." The allusion invites a comparison between Carl and the knight of the poem and between Jean and the "Faery Child." In total effect, it helps to define the love relationship between Carl and Jean, and it makes a comment upon how an individual achieves a separate, individual unity.

The second allusion is to Whitman's "Out of the Cradle Endlessly Rocking." It too comes in a comment made by Carl, this time immediately after his race under Tensquare with Jean: "Into the cradle endlessly rock-

48

ing, I spit" (DF, p. 19). In reflecting on Davits' mood at the time, it also makes a comment on their relationship and upon the maturation process. It forces a comparison between Carl and the speaker of the poem, who finds that death of individual existence releases emotional tension. It suggests that the death of ego will bring the birth of a new, mature personality.

The third allusion is to Ezra Pound's *Cantos*. They come in the use of specific descriptive phrases applied to Jean which are drawn from the following passage in the Second Canto:

> Seal sports in the spray-whited circles of cliff-wash,
> Sleek head, daughter of Lir,
>   eyes of Picasso
> Under black fur-hood, lithe daughter of Ocean. (6)

The use of "sleek head," "daughter of Lir," and "eyes of Picasso" clearly establish the link between Jean and the sporting seal in Pound's passage. By association, however, Jean is linked to other females in the *Cantos*, all of whom are "man destroyers." In the course of Pound's work, however, they evolve to become women-as-creator. This is, of course, the nature of Jean's role in "Doors," and the reference, therefore, amplifies her purpose in the novelette.

Like many of Zelazny's works, "Doors" can be read at many levels. It is the story of man's search for maturity. It is a search for love. It is a search for a state of mental health. It is a comment about failure and success. It is an adventure about the ultimate hunt. In the last analysis, it is all of these and more, for it touches that core of experience which is common to all men. Perhaps its greatest asset lies in its ability to summon for its readers those emotions, ideas, and sensations which combine to make up our personalities and thus to remind us of our humanity.

1. Theodore Sturgeon, "Introduction," in *Four for Tomorrow* by Roger Zelazny (New York: Ace Books, 1973), p. 9.
2. Roger Zelazny, "Unpublished Letter," July 25, 1974.
3. Ibid.
4. Robert Heilman, *This Great Stage: Image and Structure in King Lear* (Baton Rouge, LA: University Press, 1948), pp. 11-12.
5. Ibid., pp. 18-19.
6. Ezra Pound, *The Cantos of Ezra Pound* (New York: New Directions, 1970), p. 6.

VI.

THE DREAM MASTER

The Dream Master is yet another Zelazny novel which earned fame under a different title. Originally published as "He Who Shapes" in the January and February, 1965, issues of *Amazing*, it won a Nebula that year for best novella. It is typical early Zelazny in its reliance on mythic and literary sources to shape a traditional literary motif.

While it draws on such varied authors as Whitman, Dante, Jung, and Tennyson, it is broadly a Faust story well-seasoned with Tristan and Isolde and the Scandinavian myth of *ragnarok*. It must be noted that *The Dream Master* is not the retelling of any of these stories. Rather, they are used to provide elements which help to develop the novel's main theme—man's attempt to play God, which, in turn, leads to his own destruction.

The Dream Master is essentially the story of Charles Render, a neuroparticipation therapist, or in the vernacular, a Shaper, who has a tragic flaw. Shapers are psychiatrists who treat their patients' neuroses by controlling their dreams. Through the use of a machine called a "ro-womb," they program their patients through a series of fantasies which ultimately rebuild a healthy mental state.

Since the book makes its point primarily through its characterization, an analysis of both Render and Eileen Shallot is in order.

Though we know almost nothing about Render physically, except that he is athletic because he skis difficult slopes, we do know a great deal about him psychologically. He is skillfully unfolded through his desires, attitudes, motives, and actions.

We know that he is very difficult to please because he expects perfection. He moves his son, Peter, almost irrationally from school to school. He refuses to accept the reality that no one could have prevented the boy from breaking his ankle, choosing to blame his academy instead.

He is terribly preoccupied with death, admitting that the suicide of James Irizarry, a man he did not even know, bothered him more than it should have. Moreover, his concern with the deaths of his wife and daughter nine years earlier in an automobile accident is neurotic. He seems to have to remind himself of his own mortality by hanging on desperately to the memory of that event. He frequently pulls out a picture of Ruth, Miranda, Peter, and himself to look at it.

We also know that though he always appears to be in control, he is extremely vulnerable psychologically. In relating an incident when a patient got control of the fantasy that Render had constructed for him, he admits, " 'I did an awful lot of skiing five years ago. This is because I was a claustrophobe. I had to run and it took me six months to beat the thing—all because of one tiny lapse that occurred in a measureless fraction of an instant' " (DM, p. 33).

We know too that he believes that he has inured himself to his feelings. "It was after the auto wreck, after the death of Ruth and of Miranda, their daughter," he recalls, "that he had begun to feel detached" (DM, p. 15). What he interprets as control, however, is nothing more than the repression of very strong emotions, which eventually lead him to self-betrayal.

Finally, we know that he is arrogant, and this is his tragic flaw. He feels that he is above the normal rules and therefore fails to heed the danger signals in his analysis of Eileen. Even after a warning by Bartelmetz, his former teacher and the world's foremost neuroparticipation therapist, Render continues with his attempt to teach Eileen sight. To Bartelmetz's question as to whether she has yet taken control of a fantasy from him, Render answers, " 'She has become dominant on several occasions, but I've succeeded in resuming control almost immediately. After all, I *am* master of the bank' " (DM, p. 13).

Using a typical technique, Zelazny expands Render's characterization by linking him to several mythic and dramatic heroes. These references add dimension to the characterization and create an open-ended quality to the story. They are presented in the book through the "Act A Myth Club" sequences and the abbreviated stage pieces. The psychological basis for using them like this comes from Jung and is presented by Render himself as he prepares his paper on autopsychomimesis. He writes:

> Carl Jung pointed out that when consciousness is repeatedly frus-trated in a quest for values it will turn its search to the unconscious; failing there, it will proceed to quarry its way into the hypothetical collective unconscious. He noted in the postwar analyses of ex-Nazis, that the longer they searched for something to erect from the ruins of their lives—having lived through a period of classical icon-oclasm, and then seen their new ideals topple as well—the longer they searched, the further back they seemed to reach into the collective unconscious of their people. Their dreams themselves came to take on patterns out of the Teutonic mythos (DM, p. 58).

Ironically, Render's own search for values is progressing through the same pattern he described for the ex-Nazis. This is confirmed in another passage from his paper:

> "The point I wish to make, however, is that we are often unaware of our own values. We cannot honestly tell what a thing means to us until it is removed from our life-situation. If an object of value ceases to exist, then the psychic energies which were bound up in it are released. We seek after new objects of value in which to invest . . . " (DM, p. 57).

Render himself has suffered such a loss of value, when Ruth and Miranda were killed, so he seeks new values for his energies. Because of his own peculiarities, however, he cannot find satisfaction in the conscious world, so he is sent searching first into the unconscious and finally into the collective unconscious. The very nature of his work—the shaping of dreams—is an indication of his desire to escape the conscious world and a sign that he has reached the collective unconscious.

What he finds in the collective unconscious are archetypes, or original models, after which similar things are patterned. Archetypes are symbols of common human experience.

It is therefore logical that Zelazny would use the "Myth Club" sequences to reflect the states of mind of his characters and to underscore what is happening or about to happen to them.

Render himself is linked to several mythic characters: Orpheus, Aeneas, Abelard, Daedalus, Orestes, Tithonus, and Phaeton. Though the implication of each comparison differs, all of them generally foreshadow Render's fate. Orpheus is torn apart by Thracian maidens, Aeneas causes Dido's death because he does not return her love, Abelard is emasculated because of a woman, Daedalus is trapped by King Minos because of his pride, Orestes goes mad and is pursued by furies, Tithonus is trapped in an aged body and goes mad, and Phaeton is shot out of the sky by Jove's thunderbolt, the victim of his own pride.

Eileen's characterization is handled by the same technique. In particular, she is linked to the Lady of Shalott, in Tennyson's poem of the same name. Even though her last name is spelled differently, there are several similarities between the two. Both view the world through a mirror. Neither sees it directly. In Eileen's case, the mirror is figuratively Render.

Both women wrestle with the problem of adjusting to the larger world, fail, and are destroyed in the process. The Lady of Shalott dies, and Eileen loses her mind.

For each woman, a new love serves to carry her beyond her isolation. Not only does Eileen love Render, he almost becomes a god to her. She calls him "Life," "the Shaper," "the Maker and the Mover," "greater than heroes," "the poles of the world," "all actions" and "more than any one thing," (DM, p. 95). He opens the world of sight to her and thus carries her out of the shadows.

Finally, like the Lady of Tennyson's poem, the love is unfulfilled. Shalott dies before Lancelot even gets a chance to know her. In Eileen's case, Render is certainly attracted to her, but he is too involved with the memory of his wife, Ruth, Peter's problems, and his relationship with Jill to enter into a meaningful and psychologically healthy love relationship with her.

The failure of their relationship is underlined by the numerous references to other ill-fated love affairs. Though the circumstances of each pair of lovers is different from that of Eileen and Render, they have in common the fact that they all end in disaster. In addition to the Lady of Shalott and Lancelot, there are also Orpheus and Eurydice, Heloise and Abelard, Apollo and Daphne, and Tristan and Isolde.

From the novel, we get a full picture of Eileen, both physically and psychologically. She is in her early-thirties, she has shoulder-length bronze hair; vivid sea-green eyes; a narrow waist; long legs; large, pointed breasts; and she is blind. She wears a silver spot on her forehead, which is a miniature photoelectric cell that transmits vibrations to her brain, but it does not permit her to pick up forms. She is associated with the color green, which is also the color of the emerald from which Melchisadek, the High Priest of Israel, carved the Grail as the story is related by Render. The color symbol links Eileen to the Grail and calls up the images of all the Grail knights who sought it and failed.

Psychologically, we know that she is tough, determined, intelligent, lonely, courageous, and mentally unstable. She suffers from sight-anxiety. Even though Render believes differently, the outcome of the story proves that her ego is not strong enough to resist the radical alteration of her self-concept which comes about through the trauma of her therapy. In the end, she loses her mind, takes control of the fantasy, and draws Render into its madness with her.

As mentioned earlier, *The Dream Master* is full of myth and literary lore which give it dimension by supporting the main theme in various ways. Several of these have already been mentioned. One of the most important of them is the myth of Tristan and Isolde which is introduced in the last sequence of the novel as the fantasy in which Render is trapped.

It is a logical but unfortunate choice. It is unfortunate because it tends to confuse rather than clarify. This confusion results from the fact that there are so many versions of the story. The full impact of the allusion thus tends to diffuse rather than focus the conclusion of the novel.

Zelazny probably means to imply a kind of abstraction of the myth rather than any particular version, despite the fact that at the beginning of Chapter IV, he has the guidebook for Winchester Cathedral describe it as " . . . an appropriate setting for some tale out of Malory" (DM, p. 110). (In his last participation session with Eileen, Render recreates the Cathedral for her, and this triggers her madness.) The reason that I say that Zelazny problably has some abstraction of the myth in mind is because the black and white sails which are elements in so many variations of the story, and which are part of the final sequence of the novel, do not appear in the Malory version.

Because the Tristan myth is contained in Malory, however, it provides an excellent connection with the general Arthurian lore that permeates the novel and represents Eileen's point of view. She would like to escape from her dark world to a better one, and when she finally does have her way, she chooses a world full of chivalry, romance, fair maidens, and knights.

The Arthurian lore is used to shape the concepts of the novel and is introduced into it quite early, first appearing when Render meets Eileen at the "Partridge and Scalpel." She is sitting at a small table which is "partly masked by an ancient suit of armor" (DM, p. 20). It is thus connected with her. It is no accident that she later places him in the same suit when she briefly takes control from him during their initial participation session and that her associations with him become chivalric or courtly.

Other material supports her "Arthurian" point of view. Her very name, Shallot, recalls this lore by its association with Lancelot, and several details of the last Winchester Cathedral scene bear out the same contention. She makes the organ play "Greensleeves" and dresses herself as a knight's lady, with her slippers, gown and cone-shaped hat trailing wisps of veil. The step from here to the Tristan and Isolde fantasy is thus a logical one.

One of the goals that Zelazny set for himself in *The Dream Master* was to create " . . . a triangle situation, two women and one man. . . . " (1) He does just that, but with a typical wrinkle. To the three living figures of Jill, Eileen, and Render, he adds Ruth, the dead wife.

Ruth's role is crucial. She provides the basis for Render's neurosis. Because of his fixation with her death, he is unable to enter into a healthy love relationship with either Jill or Eileen. Moreover, it triggers the complex which makes him psychologically vulnerable.

Eileen's role is to provide the object for his aspirations. She is the challenge which his pride will not let him reject. He knows full-well the dangers of the therapy and even recognizes the signs that it is not progressing smoothly. He ought to be scared away by her constant efforts to seize control from him during the participation sessions, but he is not. He chooses to ignore the danger.

Jill's role is purely a mechanical one. She provides Render with a sex object. He reveals his feelings about her in a comment he makes to Eileen. He says that he has no intention of marrying Jill. Early in the novel, he also admits that she is growing, "if anything, more interesting to him" (DM, p. 16). This is not the comment of a man deeply in love. That Jill is a sex object is confirmed by the fact that she is associated with the colors red and white. Her Christmas present from Render is a white ermine coat upon which red punch is spilled. These are traditional *carpe diem* colors.

In the Tristan and Isolde myth, Zelazny found an analogue to help him structure his triangle relationship. Though he has altered it considerably to suit the requirements of his story, there is no question but what he means for us to make the connection between it and the novel because Render becomes Tristan in the last fantasy, and Eileen is associated with Isolde of the White Hands in their very first therapy session. Just after arriving in the glen that he creates for her, he permits his mind to wander and experiences " . . . a momentary doubling of vision, during which time he saw an enormous hand riding in an aluminum carriage toward a circle of white" (DM, p. 52). The "white" and "hand" images are unmistakable.

Confirmation is found in the similar roles that Eileen and Isolde of the White Hands play in the destruction of their lovers. Isolde consciously deceives Tristan when she tells him that the sails on the ship in the harbor are black when they are actually white. His hope gone, he dies. Whether jealous or simply ignorant, whether she intends to kill Tristan or not, the fact remains that her lie causes his death.

The significant difference, on the other hand, occurs in the fact that Eileen has no control over the events which produce Render's madness.

What happens is the product of determinism. His own vulnerability, plus his pride, combine with Eileen's sight anxiety to drive them towards an inevitable end.

There can be no other logical conclusion, for like Tristan, Render has a wound which needs healing. Whereas Tristan's is physical and the power to heal it lies with Isolde the Fair, Render's is psychological and the power to heal lies with Ruth. She is dead though, which prevents any other outcome to the story except his fall.

A second myth which Zelazny relies upon to help shape his novel is that of *ragnarok*. Translated variously as "the fatal destiny of the gods" and "twilight of the gods," (2) it is the story of inevitable doom. No matter what precautions the gods take, it is ordained that they shall fail and that their failure will bring the end of the created world.

As with the Tristan myth, Zelazny borrows certain elements from the *ragnarok* to develop his story. Render is, for example, paralleled with Odin, even though the god's name is never mentioned in the book. We are led inductively to this conclusion by other parallels between the myth and Zelazny's novel. Three, in particular, establish the association.

First, Render has a son named Peter, who breaks his ankle and must wear a cast upon it. With a little imagination, a cast could be viewed as a special type of shoe. Odin has a son named Vidar, which rhymes with Peter, who wears a special shoe that he will use to slay the Fenrir wolf after it kills his father. Vidar is destined to be one of the few figures who survives the destruction of the world and along with his brother Vali will appear in the new creation. (3) He will, thus, carry the promise of Odin into the future. Peter will likewise carry the promise of Render into the future and make his mark in the new age. It is significant that he wants to chronicle the exploration of the "Outer Five" planets and beyond.

Second, Odin's ancient enemy and destined slayer is Fenris (or Fenrir), a wolf. Fenris is mentioned by name in the novel and is associated with other wolves and dogs. All strike fear into Render. Fenris becomes the symbol of Render's destruction, appearing in the middle of the last fantasy to eat the corpses of his wife and daughter before transforming into the two-headed giant, Thaumiel.

Third, Odin is "swallowed up" by Fenris and thus meets his death. Render too is swallowed up. Though he does not literally die, his sanity is "swallowed up" by the immense energy generated when Eileen loses her mind. The image is appropriate, for it is well-supported in the novel. Render speaks of the "vacuum" in Eileen's mind "in the place where sight ought to be" (DM, p. 56), and in describing what will happen if Render breaks a *skanda*, or psychological complex, Bartelmetz says, " . . . it will be like breaking through the bottom of a pond. A whirlpool will result, pulling you—where?" (DM, p. 131). So, Zelazny's choice of destruction for Render is metaphorically comparable to Odin's.

But these are not the only parallels between the myth and the novel. In the myth, the final destruction is preceded by a mighty winter that will last for three years. *Dream Master* is set in winter, and the swirling images of snow and cold are associated with death in Render's mind:

> He could remember a time when he had loved snow . . . In his mind now, though, there was another element from which it could never be wholly disassociated. He could visualize so clearly the eddies of milk-white coldness that swirled about his old manual-steer auto, flowing into its fire-charred interior . . . and he knew, whenever he looked upon falling snow, that somewhere skulls were whitening (DM, p. 18).

One other important element that Zelazny adapts from the myth is that of the wolf swallowing the moon. This act is a sign of *ragnarok* in the myth, and in the novel it bears a similar symbolic significance.

Zelazny alters Snorri Sturluson's version of the myth slightly to make it fit his story. Snorri tells of two wolves, Fenris and Moon-Hound, who swallow the sun and the moon respectively, but Zelazny has quite logically associated the moon with Eileen. It is an extrinsic symbol of the feminine principle and has been for ages through its association with Semele, Ishtar, and Astarte. (4) He refers to the photoelectric cell on her forehead in moon terms, for example. By combining the two wolves into one and associating Eileen with the moon, he achieves a greater efficiency than by trying to work two wolf symbols into the story. When he writes "It [the Fenris wolf] leapt into the air. It swallowed the moon" (DM, p. 117), he is indicating symbolically that Eileen has met her destruction, or to be more specific, she has lost her sanity.

Like Ikky in "The Doors of His Face, the Lamps of His Mouth," Fenris also represents Render's nightmare. The wolf becomes the symbol of his mental disturbance. When he finally confronts it, however, he does not succeed in defeating it like Carlton Davits does. Rather, when he dismembers the wolf with a scalpel to keep it from eating the bodies of his wife and child (note that corpse eating is a characteristic of Moon-Hound), it transforms into the two-headed giant, Thaumiel. This is a logical transition from the mythological point of view since Snorri indicated that Moon-Hound is the child of the Witch of Ironwood, who bore "many giants for sons, and all in the shape of wolves." (5) and *Larousse* indicates that:

> Giants were able to disguise themselves; they often made use of this in their conflicts with the gods. The great serpent of the Midgard and the wolf Fenrir were, in fact, giants in disguise . . . But the best known example of metamorphosis is that of the giant Fafnir, who became a dragon to better guard his treasure. (6)

The symbol for Thaumiel is quite a complicated construction. Neither a giant nor other figure by this name appears in any of the standard mythological dictionaries. However, Qliphoth is a Cabalistic term for "the forces of evil," which would suggest that Thaumiel is out of the same tradition. Rabbi Eli Touge, of the Habbad House in Cleveland, Ohio, has suggested that Zelazny has probably adapted the Hebrew word "tamiel," which means the "perfection of God." (7) If so, and it does make sense,

Thaumiel of Qliphoth is a construction that posits both good and evil in the same being. The giant's two-headedness would reinforce that idea.

Such a construction is consistent with what we find in Zelazny's fully-developed characters, who are often drawn with the forces of both form and chaos within them. It also ties in perfectly with the legend of the origin of the Grail that Render relates to Eileen earlier in the story. Further evidence of the connection is found in the fact that he tells her that he heard the legend from a former patient named Rothman. Then, when he confronts Thaumiel, he shouts, " 'I beat you and I chained you for—Fothman, yes it was Rothman—the cabalist.' " (DM, p. 179).

His version of the Grail's origin follows:

> "The Grail was handed down by Melchisadek, High Priest of Israel, and destined to reach the hands of the Messiah. But where did Melchisadek get it? He carved it from a gigantic emerald he had found in the wilderness, an emerald which had fallen from the crown of Shmael, Angel of Darkness, as he was cast down from On High. There is your Grail, from light to darkness to light to darkness to who knows? What is the point of it all? Enantiadromia, my dear" (DM, p. 123).

"Enantiadromia (Zelazny's term: DM, p. 123) is, of course, the key to understanding his point about the Grail's origin. It means to run alternately in opposite directions, like electricity. The legend displays that characteristic. The Grail, destined for one of the forces of good, is carved from an emerald belonging to one of the forces of evil, after he has been dispelled from On High by the forces of good. It is ironic, and it is a pattern that is reflected in Render's own personality development. Because he is so disturbed by the death of his wife and daughter, he pursues a profession dedicated to healing persons with mental problems. He rises to the top of his field, yet does not realize that he needs the very same kind of help himself. Then, he succumbs to the same disease that he treats.

This "enantiadromic" pattern is supported by the sight complex of images which run through the novel. Render should "see" (in the sense of understand) better than anyone else. He has been educated to see. Yet, he is the most blind of all. As he stands looking at the wreck of the car with Fenris, he believes, about to leap upon his back and eat his brains, Zelazny writes, "He had covered his eyes, but he could not stop seeing. Not this time" (DM, p. 178).

The "not-seeing in seeing" motif is well-supported in the context of the novel. Render's behavior shows it as well as one of the allusions in the Grail-origin legend and a common myth about Odin.

The allusion is to Shmael, also Samael or Sammeal, the Angel of Darkness. According to Rabbi Touge, the word means "the blinding of God." (8) Render is accused of playing God by Minton, and though he denies it, that is exactly what he does in trying to cure Eileen.

The myth about Odin, with whom Render is associated, concerns the god's overpowering desire to drink from a fountain at the roots of the great tree, Yggdrasill, which gives secret knowledge to those who do manage to drink from it. Odin does, but the price is high—one of his eyes. Thereafter, the god appears as a one-eyed man. Even his secret knowledge cannot, however, prevent *ragnarok*. Similarly, Render's secret knowledge, which he has learned through the use of the "ro-womb," cannot prevent his inevitable destiny either.

The symbols of *The Dream Master* do an excellent job of supporting the novel's themes. In typical Zelazny fashion, they are quite complicated, but their very complexity adds dimension and richness to the story.

Some of the symbols—Fenris, Thaumiel, and the moon, for example—have already been discussed in context. Many of those remaining have been adapted from Tennyson's "Lady of Shalott." They include the willow, the river, the mirror, fire, and the color gray. Because of the complexity of these symbols in the context of the novel, no attempt will be made to completely analyze them. One example, that of the willow, will illustrate how they work.

Traditionally known as a symbol of sorrow, it is used in Tennyson's poem in this sense. It is used in *The Dream Master* in that sense also, but its meaning is considerably expanded.

The willow first appears in the novel as part of the rudimentary world that Render builds for Eileen's initial fantasy. As circumstances develop, he asks her to choose an object into which her form may flow so that she can anchor herself in the created world. She picks the willow. Later, as they return to that world time after time and an anchor is no longer necessary, she continues to use the willow as the station for her appearance. By this association, Eileen is identified not only with the willow tree but with its extrinsic meaning of sorrow as well.

This is highly appropriate for two reasons. First, it foreshadows the inevitable end of the relationship between Render and Eileen. Second, it superbly supports the final fantasy of the novel, the Tristan sequence. Render, his mind gone, is being programmed through a fantasy in which he has become Tristan. Tristan's story is one of "star-crossed lovers" fated to end badly, and the word Tristan, itself, means sorrow. So, the willow symbol comes to amplify the affair between Render and Eileen as well as to foreshadow it.

The river, the mirror, fire, and the color gray operate in similar ways. The river, associated with death, is expanded to include the lake and Render's mind. Gray is also associated with death, but in the sense of living-death. Moreover, it is connected to Render's mind, the general neurosis of society at the time of the novel, and Fenris. The mirror is likewise associated with Render's mind, but in its capacity to deceive. Fire is used to symbolize the ultimate cleansing agent. It appears with Thaumiel, and it is an important element in the *ragnarok* myth, where the final destruction is brought about by Surt, chief of the fire-giants, who "alone was left alive to fling fire over earth and heaven, so that the flames mounted as the earth sank beneath the waves." (9)

The final symbol is Render himself, for he represents Zelazny's form and chaos philosophy. A character name, "render," means to cause to be or become, to represent or depict. In other words, render means to shape, and Render is the ultimate shaper. He molds individual personalities, the "sin of the psychiatrist" in Hawthorne, for which the sinner often pays with his life.

As the ultimate shaper, Render is a strong symbol of the process Zelazny calls form, but because he is a symbol of form, he is doomed to fall, for the philosophy itself calls for the overthrow of form by chaos, and vice versa, in a never-ending process.

Like Faust, after whom Render is very broadly patterned, Render aspires too high. Both of them try to attain the unattainable. Both have mystical, magical powers (Render's in the sense that few understand neuroparticipation therapy). Both deal with the devil (Render's comes in the form of Fenris-Thaumiel, which is the product of his own mind), and both encounter the devil at one time or another in the form of a dog or wolf.

It is difficult to push the comparisons much beyond the superficial level, however, for the differences are greater than the similarities. Like the Tristan myth, there are simply too many variations of the Faust myth to permit easy interpretation. One of these occurs in the ending itself. In Goethe's version, Faust is saved at the last second and carried off to heaven where he will be reunited with Gretchen. In Marlowe's version, on the other hand, Faust loses his wager with the devil and is whisked off to hell and eternal damnation.

In the last analysis, the novel presents some of the very best of Zelazny and some of the most confusing. The reader is damned if he knows too much and damned if he knows too little. The use of the Faust and Tristan legends, with their many variations, not only opens up the novel to many possible interpretations but poses contradictory ones. Though allusions by definition invite comparisons and though Zelazny uses them very effectively most of the time, there must be enough correspondence to prevent confusion. It is a question of degree.

Nonetheless, the theme of the novel is both universal and modern. The world is imaginatively rich. Render and Eileen are characters which the reader can relate to and understand. These virtues make *The Dream Master* worth the reading.

1. Roger Zelazny, "Author's Choice," *The Alien Critic*, 2, No. 4, [Whole Number 7] November 1973, 41.
2. Pierre Grimal, ed., *Larousse World Mythology* (London: The Hamlyn Publishing Group, 1969), p. 395.
3. H. R. Ellis Davidson, *Scandinavian Mythology* (London: The Hamlyn Publishing Group, 1969), p. 109.
4. Carl G. Jung, *Man and His Symbols* (New York: Dell Publishing Company, 1975), p. 330.
5. Snorri Sturluson, *The Prose Edda*, trans. Arthur Gilchrist Brodeur (London: The Oxford University Press, 1916), p. 24.
6. Grimal, p. 395.
7. Rabbi Eli Touge, "Unpublished Letter," July 1977.
8. Touge.
9. Davidson, p. 122.

VII.

LORD OF LIGHT

When *Lord of Light* was published in 1967, it was hailed as a brilliant new science fiction novel. That verdict was upheld in 1968 when it won the Hugo. Now, more than a decade later, it remains not only Zelazny's best novel but also his most complex and most difficult.

The book makes exceptional demands of its readers. And though it can be read at the action level quite satisfactorily, a full understanding of it requires a broad knowledge of both Hinduism and Buddhism, their philosophies, terminologies, and mythologies, as well as some understanding of the historical relationship between the two. That is an extraordinary request. The problem presented by the Hindu mythology alone is illustrated by the following comment:

> The stories of gods, demi-gods, demons, sages, and heroes overlap and form such a tangled web that not only is it impossible to isolate one story alone, but none can be understood except in light of the others. Scholars have almost always beaten a weary retreat, declaring that the texts are foolish and childish in spite of some fine flights of poetry. (1)

Moreover, it is helpful to a full understanding of the novel if one knows how Zelazny works: his themes, his symbols, his ideas. With that additional knowledge, it is indeed possible to see what he has done with the material he has adapted.

In the final analysis, *Lord of Light* is a story about the reformation of a society which has gone stagnant from the weight of its rules, regulations, institutions, and concepts. Because of that stagnation, the society has lost its vitality, has become corrupt, and exploits the majority of its citizens.

As with many of Zelazny's stories, the philosophical basis for the novel comes from his ideas about form and chaos, the two dynamic and opposed forces which are eternally at work in the universe and which are reflected in all life. Form is best explained as the creative urge, the desire to shape, the compulsion to synthesize. It is the process of taking diverse and disconnected raw materials and producing new products from them. Chaos is its opposite. It is the process of tearing down, of analyzing, of destroying.

Form and chaos are mutually supportive forces, form providing the objects for chaos to break down and chaos providing the raw materials for form to shape. Together, they create a never-ending cycle which we recognize as change, and together, they produce a rhythm which underlies the actions of the universe. Man should live in as close harmony with that rhythm as possible. If he does, he will find peace, happiness, and self-realization. If not, counterforces will form in his own mind, which become psychological complexes. If he does, he will grow under the guidance of his own experience. If he does not, he will stagnate, the one condition which form and chaos will not tolerate.

No moral judgments attach to form and chaos. They are the product of men, who deem things and acts good or bad within the context of particular situations. Form and chaos simply are. They are necessary to the business of the universe.

Within the philosophy, however, there is a kind of law of conservation. Things once formed resist destruction and vice versa. Examples of this are found in the new growth of plants and in plastic memory, the tendency of plastic products once shaped to want to return to their original forms when heated. The resistances of both forces create a natural and perpetual tension in all things and actions.

In the relationship between Hinduism and Buddhism, Zelazny found a perfect metaphor for his own doctrine. The parallels between the historical relationship of the two great religions and the novel are obvious. Buddha found Hinduism to be static and corrupt, weighed down by its own dead and meaningless ritual, insensitive to the common man, and too complex to be understood by him. (2) Sam, the protagonist of *Lord of Light*, found the Hindu system of the novel, that is "deicratism" (Zelazny's term for god governed politics) to be the same. Buddha's mission on Earth was to reform the old religion, not to start a new one. Sam's mission in the novel is identical, to reform the old religion through Accelerationism. Both men are instruments of change.

In the Hindu "Trimurti," moreover, Zelazny found the perfect expression for the dynamic interaction between form and chaos. Traditionally, Brahma represents the creative forces of the universe, and Siva, its destructive forces. Vishnu, the third god of the trimurti, preserves the conditions of the universe so that the other two can interact. Also, traditionally, Brahma and Siva are born from Vishnu, and the other gods of the Hindu pantheon are drawn from these three. (3)

In the novel, it is no accident that by the time the story nears its conclusion Brahma and Siva have been destroyed and Vishnu rules in heaven. This is a metaphoric statement of the fact that one age is about to end and another is about to begin. It should be noted that Hinduism is eternally optimistic, recognizing a never-ending cycle of creations.

With the onset of the new age, or *yuga*, both the creative and destructive principles will be operating once more. They may bear different names, be immersed in different cultures, or be represented in different systems, but their function will remain the same, for they are constants.

Within the general theme of reformation are several important and supportive subordinate themes: liberation, immortality, love, vanity, guilt, and sacrifice.

Of these, the liberation theme is one of the most important because it is the basis for Sam's motivation. It is also the source for the plot actions in the story. Everything that occurs is generated from Sam's desire to free the masses from the oppressive rule of the reigning gods and those forces which oppose him. He indicates this in his reply to Rudra when asked why he had murdered Siva and Brahma:

I decided that mankind could live better without gods. If I disposed of them all, people could start having can openers and cans to open again, and things like that, without fearing the wrath of Heaven. We've stepped on these poor fools enough. I wanted to give them a chance to be free, to build what they wanted (LL, p. 198).

The strength of his conviction is borne out by a few basic facts: 1) he initially takes on the resources of Heaven and the gods virtually alone; 2) he is willing to murder to accomplish his ends, even though as Lord Siddhartha Sam supported the Buddhist doctrine of *ahisma*, which states that man should refrain from harming life of any kind; 3) he triggers the battle of Keenset, as a result of which he is "killed" by being dispersed into the magnetic cloud which surrounds the planet; and 4) even after he is returned from *nirvana* by Yama, he triggers a second battle at Khaipur, thus risking his life once more.

Several questions immediately come to mind regarding the liberation themes, such as how it relates to the form and chaos philosophy, how it relates to the Hindu and Buddhist sources, and how it is treated and supported in the novel.

In relating the form and chaos philosophy to liberation, it is first necessary to understand how Zelazny views systems. He believes that as they age, they lose momentum in the process of becoming more sophisticated. Thus, they become more restrictive and repressive. Eventually, they become static.

This stasis prevents the growth of the system itself and of those individuals who are involved in it. Men sense that the system is out of harmony with the natural rhythm of the universe, and they move to change it. When they do, they become instruments for chaos. Liberation is the human side of destruction. It is the freeing of man from the repressiveness of a system which has no meaning for him. This is a necessary act if man is to grow.

Moreover, the liberation theme finds a parallel in the Hindu and Buddhist concept of self-realization. Briefly stated, it is the goal of man to continue to grow so that he can eventually reach such a high state of consciousness that he can merge with the Absolute. Man undergoes reincarnation as many times as necessary to gain the experiences which will free him from the bonds of worldly existence. (4)

In a well-crafted novel, all parts—that is sub-themes, actions, and characters—should support the main theme of the story and each other. In other words, nothing in the novel should be extraneous. Each element should develop the basic purpose. *Lord of Light* is such a novel, with each part playing a role in the unfolding of the whole. For this reason, only the major devices which support the liberation theme will be discussed here. Foremost among these is Accelerationism. It is a doctrine of sharing, which proposes that Heaven give those who dwell below its powers, knowledge, and substance. If implemented, it would raise every man to the condition of being a god, and it would destroy Heaven's exclusiveness. As a piece of the story's machinery, it provides a means for liberating the masses, and by its emphasis on technological development, the easiest way to accommodate them to rapid change. It is, in effect, a synonym for progress.

A second supporting device is the character of Sam himself. As drawn, he is a metaphor for the form and chaos philosophy. In his earliest identity, as Lord Kalkin, he is the binder of energy, a form maker in effect. He, and the others of the First, have formed the initial Earth-oriented civilization by tearing control of the planet away from its original inhabitants. Thus, in the process of forming, he destroys. Later, as Mahasamatman, he frees the demons that he bound earlier, he attacks the gods both physically and psychologically, he destroys the prevailing political system, and he brings down the machinery of Heaven. He has become destroyer once more. As characterized, he represents the endless cycle of creation and destruction.

Sam functions as liberator twice over. First, he is instrumental in freeing the planet so that its Hindu-based society can be formed. Later, he frees the First's descendants from Deicratism. He is both the symbol of liberation and the device of its implementation.

Yet another device to support the liberation theme is found in the symbol of light. Light is synonymous with illumination, and illumination, in turn, with the Hindu and Buddhist concept of self-realization. The goal of man is to perfect himself, rising through various levels of consciousness to illumination where he will become aware of eternal truth and thus be liberated from the illusion and ignorance of the world.

It must also be noted that Sam is referred to as the "Lord of Light." Though there are various lords of light in Hindu and Buddhist lore, it is clear that Zelazny is associating him with Maitreya, the Buddha of the Future. Maitreya is the Sanskrit word for love and refers to that Buddha who will come to reform mankind through the power of his divine love. (5)

Two clues indicate this connection. At the beginning of Chapter vii, Sam is identified for the first time as "Maitreya, Lord of Light," which also indicates the role that he has assumed. In Buddhist lore, Maitreya's appearance signals the end of the current age, the *Kali Yuga*, also known as the Age of Iron or the Age of Darkness. In Hindu lore, the end of the *Kali Yuga* is marked by the appearance of Kalki, the tenth avatar of Vishnu. Kalki is known as "the white horse" avatar, and is portrayed in myth as riding a white horse and "wielding a sword which will blaze like a comet, to create, renew, and restore purity on earth." (6) It is significant that Sam is known as Lord Kalki(n) in one identity and that he appears at the battle of Khaipur (which marks the final defeat of the "Deicrats") riding a white horse.

Though immortality is one of the recurrent themes of Zelazny's work and though it is extremely important in *Lord of Light*, its principal function in this novel is to support the liberation theme. At the surface level, it does this by providing a means for keeping the self alive through the body transfer machines. This is necessary so that Sam has enough time to mature. At the philosophical level, it provides the time necessary for an individual to develop to a state of illumination. Only the accumulation of experience and continued awareness of past identities can provide the necessary information because Zelazny has made immortality the product of technology. This removes the guarantee of immortality that the individual receives through reincarnation in Hindu and Buddhist thinking. It also permits the Deicrats to use it to control the masses by blackmailing them into obeying their wishes. It is the repression that comes from the blackmailing that moves Sam to free the masses.

The love theme too supports liberation. Generally Zelazny views love as a means for man to explore himself. Most of the time, a love relationship brings the individual new perceptions about himself which lead to a transformation of personality. Gallinger, in "A Rose for Ecclesiastes," and Davits, in "The Doors of His Face, the Lamps of His Mouth," are excellent examples of the impact of love on the individual. The transformation process is in itself liberating because it can only occur when the individual has freed himself from those psychological restrictions which bind him. In Zelazny's work, it is vanity which he must most often overcome.

Love of humanity is the specific trigger for Sam's desire to liberate the masses. When he becomes Maitreya, he has matured beyond the mere matter of male-female love. Candi/Kali/Brahma does not, of course, understand this. Though there was a time when their love was important to both of them, Sam has outgrown it. In the very touching scene in section v, when Kali and Sam recall their past love; Sam insists that they are no longer the same two people they once were, that they have changed. Kali disagrees, and the truth of the matter is that she may be right. Though he has changed greatly, her actions and attitudes imply that she may not be much different than she was in that earlier time.

In his relationship with Kali, Sam reflects the historical Buddha, who left his wife and home to pursue enlightenment, and their relationship also reflects the endless cycle of form and chaos. Sam suggests this in his comment to her, ' "Lady, Lady, Lady, forgive me . . . Our days are past, and I do not wish to recall them. They were good, but they are past. As there is a time for everything, there is a time also for the end of everything.' " (LL, p. 157).

Clearly Sam has progressed beyond the needs of the individual relationship. When he takes the field at Khaipur, it is because he is now a lover of mankind, and what he does to save them is a matter of cosmic necessity.

Vanity is another recurrent Zelazny theme which finds a place in *Lord of Light*. As mentioned earlier, it most often appears as the barrier to an individual's psychological development. Such is the case in this novel, particularly with the gods. It is vanity which prevents Kali from maturing along with Sam. It is her pride which makes her break her marriage contract with Yama to become Brahma. Yama too is a proud and arrogant man. Sam uses exactly those terms to describe him after he has tricked the death-god into stepping into quicksand. And, the other gods are also characterized as vain. Brahma/Madeline is preoccupied with his/her sexuality, and the "Deicrat" attitude towards the common man is equally proud. They have taken away all of his prerogatives for decision. They shape his life; they protect him from dangerous ideas and inventions; they play "god" with him.

Pride is the corrupting factor for most of the novel's characters, and it is from pride that Sam must liberate them. This point of view is consistent with traditional Hinduism and Buddhism. It was the pride and insolence that the historical Buddha found among the Hindu priests of his time that prompted his reform. Joseph Politella writes,

> These were the truths which the Brahmans had apparently lost; or which, holding for themselves, had kept enlightenment from the other castes, thus causing them to fall into blindness and ignorance by sheer neglect—or worse, by spiritual pride and insolence. (7)

It is obvious from this comment that Zelazny modeled his "Deicrats" along the lines of the Brahman priests of Buddha's time.

Like those already discussed, the guilt theme also supports the liberation theme and the form and chaos philosophy. Guilt is a distinctly human condition. This is shown when Taraka, a demon, invades Sam's body after being freed from Hellwell. During the possession, Taraka learns guilt and finds that once having learned it, he is bound in a prison even more terrible than that from which he had just been released.

Zelazny attributes guilt to the constant warring of intellect with emotion, will with desire, ideals with environment. The friction between these dichotomies creates a state in man where he can never be sure that his acts are completely right or wrong, completely successes or failures. Because absolutes are denied him, doubt intervenes and with doubt comes guilt. Guilt can be explained as man being out of harmony with the natural rhythms of the universe. Man is after all part of nature himself, and as such, the natural rhythms of form and chaos, from which all other dichotomies are spun, flow through him. Most of the time, he blocks the flow of these forces from his consciousness by his fixation on earthly things. Subsequently, he remains unconscious of the genesis of his guilt, even though he feels the disharmony at a subliminal level. If he placed greater trust in his intuitions, he would become more aware of those natural rhythms and promote his own psychological growth.

In the novel itself, Sam admits that the reason it took him so long to move against the corrupt "Deicrat" system was because of his own guilt, (LL, p. 136). After all, he had been party to establishing the system in the first place. He had taken a leading role in tearing a world loose from chaos and in building the first city of men. He knew Heaven as it now was, but he remembered how it was originally dreamed.

The characters of *Lord of Light* are handled as superbly as its themes. They are well drawn, they are believable, and they support the purpose of the novel. Most of them find their genesis in the traditional gods and goddesses of Hinduism and Buddhism, but Zelazny has altered them drastically, in some cases, to suit the needs of his story. The status of some has been upgraded, that of others, downgraded. Functions, where appropriate, have been changed completely or made more specific. The following

65

examples will illustrate.

Lord Nirriti, though not a major figure, is an important one in the book. As the malcontent ex-Chaplain of *The Star of India*, the starship which brought the First from Earth, he has not only left Heaven but wages war against it with an army of zombies. He represents Christianity and symbolically makes a statement about it.

Yet, in Hindu mythology, he is a rather minor figure. Nirriti, which means "non-right," is most often pictured as a goddess of darkness and evil who presides over the physical decay which precedes death and rides on the back of a man. (8) Occasionally, he/she is a rudra and a lokapala (aggressive spirits or elementals) of the southwest direction. Clearly Zelazny has upgraded the character to make his statement about Christianity.

Other gods are downgraded. Agni, a major Hindu deity representing divine will or conscious power, (9) is hardly significant in the novel. The status of still others is changed completely.

Kubera is such a case. As a Vedic god, he is chief of all evil beings. Carried over to the Hindu period, he is a god but remains king of the yaksha demons. (10) In the Buddhist pantheon, he becomes Buddha's bodyguard, also named Jambhala. (11) Yet, in the novel, he is a warm person, sympathetic to Sam, who eventually fights with him at both the battles of Keenset and Khaipur. He represents good, and he performs the important function of whisking Sam away from Heaven before Yama can kill him after Sam has murdered Brahma/Madeline and the first Siva.

In *Lord of Light*, we encounter a favorite Zelazny technique—the gathering of several identities around one person. Sam is, for example, also Lord Kalkin, Buddha, Maitreya, Tathagatha, Siddhartha, and Manjusri. Kali is also Candi, Durga, Brahma, and Murga. This technique serves two purposes. First, it enables immortals or near-immortals to protect themselves from the rest of society, to retain their privacy, or to make new beginnings. Second, it indicates an expansion of personality, a growth, with each new identity adding to and enriching the original character.

The extra identities are usually always mythological or literary, but they may also be religious or historical. Always, they bear a core of similarity to the character they amplify. The identities which cluster around Sam, for example, are either incarnations of Vishnu, or various names for Buddha, who is himself considered to be an incarnation of Vishnu.

There are three major characters in *Lord of Light*. From the actions, decisions, thoughts, desires, and motives of Sam, Kali, and Yama, the plot develops and the theme unfolds.

Sam is a typical Zelazny hero. He is a near-immortal, both physically and mentally larger than real life, a rebel against what he considers to be an unjust system, and a producer of change. He is one of the First, the original group of colonists who came to the new planet from Earth (corrupted to Urath by the time of the novel) on the *Star of India*. Though we have no permanent physical description of him because of the periodic body changing that occurs in the novel, we do know a great deal about him psychologically.

The character-name, Mahasamatman, can be translated as "Great-souled One," a perfect description of Sam, the defender of humanity, the champion of justice. Though Lady Ratri describes him as irreverent, insincere, and a charlatan, her evaluation can only be taken half-heartedly, for Sam's actions belie the harshness of those terms. He does, after all, sacrifice his own life in an attempt to bring down the "Deicrats," and he fights two wars with the gods before he succeeds in liberating the common man.

He is also described as a Machiavellian schemer. That, too, is true only to a degree. He does scheme, but with a purpose that is just. In his case, the ends do truly justify the means. He would be the philosopher king rather than the despot. He is intelligent, resourceful, active, strong-willed, loving and humane. He is extraordinarily human but remember that he has figuratively achieved enlightenment, so these characteristics are in keeping with what we would expect him to be. He is Promethean. He is an adventurer, and in the last analysis, he has lived life to its fullest, dredging every bit out of his experience that he can.

Yama, though bearing the title "God of Death," is not a villain in the standard sense, even though he set out as Sam's "Moriarity" at the beginning of the story. His characterization is probably loosely based upon the Vedic god, Visvakarma, a master artificer, who is credited with making Vishnu's discus, Siva's trident, Karttikeya's lance and the other weapons of the gods, (12) and the Satan of Milton's *Paradise Lost*. In many ways, he resembles the king of the demons, Vairocana, a sympathetic character who is pious, a respecter of holy law, and desirous of performing his role as well as he can. (13)

Two characteristics stand out in Zelazny's description of Yama. He is a technological genius, having invented the Thunder Chariot, the pray-o-mat machines, Tak's bright spear, and the machines that both disperse and reclaim Sam's *atman*, or soul, from the magnetic cloud that surrounds the planet. Second, he is very proud, like Satan. Sam-as-Buddha chides him for his pride.

He is also extremely jealous of Kali and completely enslaved by his love for her. Jan Olvegg, the ex-Captain of the *Star of India*, indicates that Yama was a third-generation, snot-nosed brat of dubious parentage who had a compulsion for souping up generators and who blew himself up at the age of sixteen. So damaged was his original body that he had to be transferred immediately to the only other body available at the time, that of a fifty-year-old man. In that sense, he was old before his time. He is an efficient and capable killer, his function by title. During the course of the novel, he eliminates Lord Mara, Siva-who-had-been-Agni, Rild-as-Sugata, and the demon Taraka, all in their own right highly efficient assassins.

Kali, who was also one of the First, is independent, beautiful, sexually desirable, intelligent, resourceful, powerful, and ambitious. She is also very proud and vengeful.

The extent of her wrath is displayed by the nature of the human sacrifice she requests on the day of her wedding to Yama. Because she was snubbed by Sam, she asks that he and Helba be hunted down by the albino tigers of Kanniburah Forest. Then, on the day of the "weird," when Mara's spell permits the barrier between the Forest and the City to be dropped so that the tigers may range freely, she turns herself into one of the huge cats, hunts down her victims, and eats them herself. Unknown to her, Sam has found a means of escaping his fate. The possession by the demon Taraka had strengthened his "flames,"--essential energy—to such an extent that he can continue to exist for a time without a body. Moreover, while in that state, he can also use his attribute of electrodirection to take over a new body being prepared for Lord Murugan.

Once Sam's lover and eventually his wife when they rode together as Durga and Lord Kalkin against the demons, Kali does not understand how he could have simply broken off their relationship and walked away from her. Because of her great pride, she feels scorned. Through the years, her love gradually turned to an all-consuming desire for revenge.

This aspect of her personality may be drawn from the "Ma Kali" or "Black Mother" myth. In that myth she is described as dancing naked, wild-eyed and dishevled, with lolling tongue, brandishing a blood-stained knife, and holding a human head dripping blood. A necklace of human heads lies upon her breast.

The necklace is interpreted to be those false personalities which must be brutally removed from each of us. They are our frailties: sin, attachment to material things, weakness. (14) If they are not removed, then, we cannot find our true identities, perfect and divine. In this role, Kali functions as purgator, helping each person free himself from the illusion of the world so that he can advance towards enlightenment. She plays a similar role in her relationship with Sam. Their stormy marriage makes him change, and makes him grow, and when he has outgrown her, he leaves.

In terms of the mechanics of the novel, Yama and Kali/Brahma alternately serve as adversary to Sam. Initially, Yama fills the role of chief antagonist with Kali serving a supporting but lesser role. When she turns her back on her marriage to Yama, however, to fulfill her insatiable ambition by accepting the role of Brahma, he becomes Sam's ally and she becomes the chief antagonist.

Of the novel's remaining characters, many simply function as foils. Strake, Vama, Simha are such examples. Others, however, play a more substantial role in the development of theme or plot. Vishnu is a case in point. Though he plays almost no part in the action of the novel, he is extremely important to its thematic development. He is the symbol of balance, and he functions traditionally as the Preserver. As such, it is his role to adjust the relationship between good and evil. Normally, in this constant battle, things are evenly matched, but when evil does get the upper hand, he incarnates and descends to Earth to restore the balance. His avatars are, therefore, not randomly selected. Each time he descends, the particular character he becomes has a specific task to perform. Significantly, after the battle of Khaipur and the defeat of the Deicratic system, he is left to rule in Heaven.

As the dichotomies of form and chaos underlie Zelazny's novel, so they underlie Hinduism and Buddhism. In describing the Hindu creation, *Larousse* says:

> ... the achievement up to this point is the mobilisation both of the basic eternal principles and of creative, divine will, which governs the forces involved. The subsequent development is that in which dualities-polarities appear, the opposed forces [in other words, the gods and the demons]. This is the substance of the myth in which Indra, king of the gods, and Vairocana, king of the demons, are jointly instructed by Brahma, and from this one lesson, each of them absorbs only what he must do in order to play the part assigned to him in the cosmos ... Once this duality—or rather polarity—of god and the devil in the world has appeared, multiplicity proper can manifest itself—not as yet the multiplicity of objects, beings, and individualized movements, but that of secondary principles that will enable the rest to come to life. (15)

The balance created by these opposed forces is fundamental to the dynamism of the universe and parallel to Zelazny's form and chaos. So, it is appropriate that Zelazny loads *Lord of Light* with images of polarity to support these concepts.

He does this quite well, which several examples will illustrate. Perhaps the most obvious symbol of polarity is found in the Celestial City. Vishnu, its creator and traditionally the Preserver, designed it so that the metropolitan area would be balanced by the wilderness of the Kanniburah Forest, all under the same dome, of course. One passage, in particular, clarifies its association with the polarity of form and chaos.

> While wilderness can exist independent of cities, that which dwells within a city requires more than the tamed plants of a pleasance. If the world were all city, he [Vishnu] had reasoned, the dwellers within it would turn a portion of it into a wilderness, for there is that within them all which desires that somewhere there be an end of order and a beginning to chaos. (LL, p. 150).

So, the balance was created: the perfect, planned city set side by side with the wild and untamed wilderness, but as with all polarities in the book, the dynamic nature of the tensions between the two poles cause the balance to eventually falter. Celestial law does not permit stasis. Appropriately, the destruction of the balance that exists under the dome is initiated by the gods themselves. The "weird" cast by Lord Mara permits the phantom cats of the Forest to roam the streets of the city. Zelazny writes:

> Vishnu was not pleased, later being quoted as having said that the City should not have been defiled with blood, and that wherever chaos finds egress, it will one day return (LL, p. 179).

Other examples of polar images are found in the opposition of "Deicratism" to Accelerationism, the demons to the humans, Yama to Sam, within the personality of Sam himself, and in the style of the narration. Frequently, Zelazny punctures the sublime with the ridiculous, creating humor. Note, for example, the very short scene between Kabada and Vama the merchant, who is collecting fecal matter so that when he is able to install one of the newly re-invented flush toilets in his home, his karmic record will show that he actually started its use eight days before, thus proving his desire for rapid advancement in life.

In addition to these polarities of concept, character, and style, the novel, as a whole, presents a counterpoint of sublime Hindu and Buddhist religious ideas set against the mechanism and technology of the First. Zelazny is ingenious in his realistic and technical explanations of reincarnation, nirvana, and other esoteric concepts. Moreover, his explanations are within the realm of technological possibility. The contrasts are delightful and refreshingly original.

Lord of Light is fated to be a science fiction classic. It is well-conceived and well-implemented. It is organic, and it is well-paced. It is humorous and sublime. Its characters are believable and sympathetic. More than any of Zelazny's other novels, it is always under tight control. Considering the morass of background material from which it was hewn, it is in the last analysis quite remarkable. It will, of course, always make severe demands of its readers, but if the effort is made, it will prove to be highly rewarding.

1. Pierre Grimal, ed., *Larousse World Mythology* (London: The Hamlyn Publishing Group, 1969), p. 209.
2. Joseph Politella, *Seven Religions* (Kent, OH: Kent State University, 1958), p. 66.
3. Grimal, p. 211.
4. Politella, p. 46.
5. W. Y. Evans-Wentz, trans., *The Tibetan Book of the Dead* (New York: Causeway Books, 1973), p. 108.
6. Politella, p. 30.
7. Politella, p. 66.
8. Veronica Ions, *Indian Mythology* (London: The Hamlyn Publishing Group, 1967), p. 32.
9. Grimal, p. 230.
10. Ions, p. 84.
11. Ibid., p. 135.
12. Grimal, p. 210.
13. Ions, p. 80.
14. Grimal, pp. 224-225.
15. Ibid., p. 210.

VIII.

HOME IS THE HANGMAN

Although Zelazny's "Home is the Hangman" is a novella of such excellence that it won both a Hugo and a Nebula in 1976 and, therefore, quite capable of standing examination on its own merits, it is better understood when placed into the context created by its two companion pieces, "The Eve of RUMOKO" and " 'Kjwalll'kje'k'koothaillll'kje'k" (hereafter referred to as "Kjwalll," for obvious reasons). These three stories have already been collected under the title of *My Name is Legion* and presently complete Zelazny's "no-name detective" series.

Each story is a mystery set in the near future and centers on a man whose real name is never given because he has no official existence. In a world where virtually everyone is catalogued in a massive computer network called the Central Data Bank, Nemo, for lack of a better name, has achieved the unique distinction of existing outside the system. By a combination of luck and brains, he has not only erased his records from the data bank but figured out how to manipulate it so that he can create identities for himself as he chooses. In this respect, Nemo resembles Zelazny's other major characters.

As with many of Zelazny's heroes, Nemo is straight out of the "Rebel" tradition. He is against a system that is too rigid and which pries too deeply into individual privacy. Yet, unlike most rebels, he does not try to destroy it. Rather, he is content to co-exist with it as long as it does not intrude upon him. So strong is his desire to maintain this relationship just as it is that he has murdered to protect his anonymity (NL, p. 61).

Despite the fact that his name remains unknown, a fairly good composite picture of Nemo can be drawn from the three stories. He is independent, resourceful, tall, blond-haired, and proficient at judo, having achieved *nidan* status in the French Federation System. He has a low violence index, knows how to hurt others, is highly intelligent, and smokes when he is puzzled. He is a trained computer programmer but can pass as a proficient technician in several other fields. He has claustrophobic tendencies, feels very guilty on occasion, and when strongly motivated will assume the role of crusader to set things right. Witness, for example, his determination to sabotage the *second* RUMOKO project to prove how dangerous they are. He is not afraid to make difficult decisions and is able to live with the burden of their ramifications. In "Kjwalll," for instance, Nemo confirms that he did, in fact, sabotage the RUMOKO project and that several persons died because of it. Yet, this does not affect his performance on subsequent cases.

This, and the fact that he stands above the system, give him godly overtones. His power comes through his ability to manipulate the Central Data Bank by means of Bill Mellings' weather station at Thule. An illegal tie-in permits him to create and destroy records, and thus to create and destroy identities as he chooses. He exercises this option when it will help him on his cases but is careful not to overuse this vast power and call attention to himself. At one point, when he is suddenly overwhelmed by this potential, he remarks, "I was damn near a god" (NL, p. 61).

Nemo is only able to continue to beat the system, however, as long as he can find work for which he can be paid in cash. He has solved that problem by working as a special agent for Don Walsh's Global Detective Agency. He takes only the most difficult assignments, either because they are too dangerous or too unique for anyone else. He works only a few times a year, receives a high salary, and protects his identity by communicating with Walsh face to face, usually by setting prearranged meeting places. He does this by sending Walsh a Christmas card on which he lists the various bars, and the dates that he will be in those bars, throughout the world: If Walsh wants him then, it is up to him to meet him there.

He is a confirmed bachelor, though he is capable of deep feelings of love. His love for Eva in "The Eve of RUMOKO" and his deep feelings for Margaret Millay, the handicapped telepath in "Kjwalll," bear this out.

He admits to bitching and moaning about progressive mechanization, to occasionally feeling certain rebellious feelings stirring deep within his psyche, and to doing stupid things, which he believes will lead him to an early grave. He has learned how to beat a lie detector and how to resist truth drugs.

Nemo is introduced in "The Eve of RUMOKO," a story set in the first decade of the twenty-first century, in a world which features the Central Data Bank, over-population, and bubble cities beneath the sea.

RUMOKO, the name of the Maori god of thunder and earthquakes, is a project to produce islands by drilling through the Earth's crust and releasing its magma by exploding atomic bombs. The magma, shooting up through the sea, will produce a volcanic island whose eco-systems will be speeded along artificially. The project, though alleged to be safe by the government scientists, is not.

So afraid are some groups, including those from the undersea cities, that attempts have been made to sabotage the project. It is at this point that Nemo enters the case, primarily because two of Walsh's best investigators disappeared under strange circumstances.

Once Nemo is on the scene, the solution unfolds rather quickly. Through a combination of luck and shrewd deduction, he manages to capture the two men responsible for the sabotage and to permit the project to proceed on schedule.

The theme of the story is man's offense against nature. Zelazny shows the fearsome results of such tampering when he describes the new volcano rising out of the sea as a kraken. A fabulous Scandinavian sea monster, the kraken's rising from the depths sounds an ominous note, for this act is alleged to foreshadow Armageddon. Zelazny does not literally mean Armageddon, but by its use he does wish to suggest the severe damage that man can cause by intruding into areas he knows little about.

Later we find out that the saboteurs had been correct. The government scientists had miscalculated the dangers of RUMOKO, and the forces released by the magma crack the dome of the undersea city of New Eden, killing thousands of its residents. One of them, Nemo has reason to believe, was Eva, a girl he had once loved and almost married. Ironically, these results justify the actions of the two saboteurs and brings Nemo into their camp.

He resolves to carry out a plan to sabotage the second RUMOKO project himself by increasing the power of the explosion to such a degree that the results of the project will terrify everyone so much that they will abandon any future attempts. We learn in "Kjwalll" that that was exactly what happened.

The RUMOKO project is an example of technology misused and illustrates one of the extreme positions in Zelazny's own view of the subject. In response to a question I once asked him about technology, he wrote:

My views on technology are kind of complicated . . . but let me kind of sketch them by first referring to a pair of books which seem . . . to represent two ways of looking at things: John McHale's *The Future of the Future* and Eugene S. Schwartz' *Overskill.* Schwartz says basically that technology is incapable of producing a genuine solution for any of the problems of the world . . . but rather that it keeps coming up with quasi-solutions which result in secondary problems that have the cumulative effect of screwing things up in the newer, more sophisticated fashions. Then, when technology is focused on this new generation of messes, the same thing occurs—more quasi-solutions, more unanticipated secondary problems—so that, eventually, the net effect is an overall loss of ground rather than a gain, and that continuing to proceed along this line is fruitless, and may ultimately prove fatal, because of the finiteness of the system within which we are working. McHale, on the other hand, builds a case to the effect that not only has mankind come up with a solution for everything that has arisen thus far (or at least an effective means of dealing with it), but that the solutions tend to evolve along with the problems, often occurring independently in other areas from whence they can be transferred. He then points to everything wrong with the cities today and the parallel development of the space program as a working out of this thesis: to wit, the establishment of techniques for astronauts' existing in the finite confines of space stations for prolonged periods of time—the balancing, recycling, etc.—as providing physical and mathematical models which will have eventual large-scale applicability when transferred to the operation of cities and various eco-systems. Schwartz and McHale seem to make the best cases I have seen thus far for both extremes. Personally, I think they are both somewhat right. On a purely pragmatic level, solutions must necessarily lag a step or so behind problems, and they are never perfect. And they do create problems of their own. I wonder about the speed involved in the process and the exhaustion potential, though. And McHale's notion does have its merits too. It has, for example, always struck me as more than coincidental that pure mathematics has preceded physics, sometimes by generations, in coming up with something of no apparent application which subsequently fits previously unknown phenomena ... Still, McHale's thesis does almost require an act of faith in a sort of mystical response of the human mind to the development of ideas and processes. Still, still again, it does seem to have occurred many times. While I am something of a mystic in my outlook on life, it is not the sort of thing one feels comfortable betting money on. And the problems do keep getting bigger and requiring grander solutions, and the pace of development has stepped up so that it does seem more and more like a race. The fact that optimism has a small edge in me makes me feel that the humans can win it, but I also think that Schwartz' thesis is valid to the extent that if more consideration is not given to the quasi-solution/residual problem effect, attention will be forced in this direction by the operation of the self-limiting factors in the world's systems. In other words, disasters great and small.

Well, I have felt this way for some time, and various bits of it have doubtless filtered through in a number of places in my writing. Like Tanner's naive metaphor of a mechanistic world in his comments on the Big Machine, when talking to the little boy in DAMNATION ALLEY, through Jack's smashing the big machine and changing the world in JACK OF SHADOWS, to a more complex working out of the situation in TODAY WE CHOOSE FACES— though actually this was not the focus of any of those books. (1)

"Rumoko" works out the Schwartz thesis quite nicely. The concern for possible disasters by the misuse of technology creates the conditions for Nemo to reverse his position, gives the reader a perception about the human condition, and supports the theme of the abuse of nature. Though man is human and, by definition, prone to error, technology gives him such power that errors are no longer possible. The paradox of his situation is inescapable.

" 'Kjwalll'kje'k'koothailll'kje'k" is the second of the Nemo stories and was written as a response to a specific question: "What might happen when rational, scientific man comes into contact with the realities of future religious experience?" (ES. dustjacket). It was originally published in *An Exaltation of Stars*, edited by Terry Carr, who wanted to find out how three science fiction writers would handle the problem of what religion might come to be under different circumstances. "Kjwalll" considers the form that spiritual ecstasy might take not only for a man but for an entirely different life form—the dolphin. (2)

Following the pattern established in "Rumoko," Nemo is called into the case by Don Walsh because it is too unique for any of his regular agents. Nemo is asked to vindicate a gang of dolphins of a homicide charge. Two scubadivers turned up dead in an undersea park in waters just off the island of Andros, the victims of what appear to be bottle-nosed dolphin bites.

The parks are undersea areas bounded by sonic walls which keep nearly everything outside that is out and everything inside that is in, except for dolphins, who have learned to operate the sonic locks on the seafloor, and man. The parks are operated and maintained by the Beltrane Company, an outfit that has built several artificial islands in the Gulf Stream for the purpose of extracting uranium from seawater. At the time old Sam Beltrane invented an economically feasible screening process (making millions from it, of course), it was good form to make some gesture of appeasement to the very powerful ecological interests. His was the parks, which permitted scientists close study of dolphins.

Once again, Nemo proceeds through the case by a combination of luck and several shrewd deductions, though this time he has the help of a deformed telepath to direct him to the necessary clues. He discovers a diamond smuggling plot, murder, betrayal, and adultery. Two divers, Mike Thornley and Paul Vallons found an underwater diamond field, and Frank Cashel, a geologist, was smuggling the stones for them. Paul, unfortunately, got "high" several times on a drug called "Pink Paradise" and told a local shady character, Rudy Myers, about their scheme. Rudy then tried to blackmail them. Mike and Paul concocted the dolphin coverup after they murdered Rudy with the jawbone from a dolphin skeleton that was in the processing station's museum. Paul, in his greed, disposed of Mike in the same way.

Later, Frank Cashel murdered Paul, whom he discovered was having an affair with his wife, Linda, by smothering him while he was recovering from the bends. When Nemo figures out who Paul's killer is, he and Frank get into a fight. In the battle, Frank gets kicked into the water and eaten by a shark that had penetrated the area while the sound wall was down for repairs.

In all, the plot is a little too contrived to be considered good, with circumstances and luck playing too great a role in its resolution. Some of what appears to be coincidence is explained away later when Margaret Millay admits that she had manipulated events to some degree to bring things to a conclusion. It must be remembered that the plot of the story is really secondary to the purpose of the story which is to explore the dolphin's religious ecstasy.

In that sphere, Zelazny's concept is excellent. He lays the groundwork for defining dolphin religious experience by first defining the dolphin mind. It is, he says, one which is capable of thinking serially while simultaneously journeying sideways in time. The sideways trips are like human daydreaming, except that they are acoustically-oriented, whereas human daydreaming is visually-oriented. Since dolphins do not sleep like humans do because of their need to go topside to breathe regularly, Zelazny postulates that their constant daydreaming releases them from the reality of second-to-second existence. Also, since the dolphin mind is acoustically-oriented, he postulates that the dolphin might splash around in the water making sound tracks in an almost never-ending, creative process.

To these physical concepts, Zelazny adds the idea that a religious experience for dolphins is a sublimination of the play instinct, which is, itself, a modification of Johan Huizinga's thesis that "culture begins as a sublimination of the play instinct . . . " (NL, p. 93).

Thus, for the dolphin, religious ecstasy is a kind of acoustical dream-song, and like men, some of them are better than others. Margaret Millay, who has experienced it, says that the greatest known to her was a dolphin named 'Kjwalll'kje'k'koothaill'kje'k, and through her telepathic abilities, she lets Nemo experience it.

As brilliant and beautiful as the dreamsong is, however, the novella itself must finally be judged as an uneven story which uses the Nemo material as background for an infinitely more sophisticated idea. The two elements do not seem to harmonize, nor to be harmonious.

Of the three stories about the "no-name detective," there is no question that "Home is the Hangman" is the best. It is paced much better than the other two. It moves swiftly and directly through the business of the story to a startling but well-prepared conclusion. It is tightly controlled in style and concept. Like the other two, it blends some interesting technological ideas with hard-hitting action to create suspense and adventure.

The Hangman is an anthropomorphic machine sent out from Earth to explore the solar system. When last heard from, some twenty years earlier, it was about to make a landing on Uranus, but at that time it seemed to undergo a breakdown similar to a human nervous breakdown.

The Hangman is a unique piece of machinery, a combination of telefactor and computer, yet greater than the sum of both. A telefactor is "a slave machine operated by remote control" (NL, p. 147) in a feed-back situation with its operator. The computer is not quite like any previous computer. Because of the development of a "superconductive tunnel junction neuristor," the Hangman's computer is an analog for the human brain. Another innovation in its technology, a very sophisticated communication device, sets up "a weak induction field in the brain of the operator," which permits him to know what is happening in the brain of the machine. The Hangman is equipped with a similar device so that two-way communications are possible. Its ability to read the mind of its operators would, it was hoped, have a humanizing effect on it. What the Hangman's inventors made was quite literally artificial intelligence, and they were rewarded when, after awhile, it was able to make its own decisions.

When Nemo enters the case, the Hangman's ship has just crashed or landed in the Gulf of Mexico, and Manny Burns, a restauranteur and one of the Hangman's four original teachers, has been found beaten to death in his New Orleans establishment, the *Maison Saint-Michel.*

Of the three remaining teachers, one, Senator Jessie Brockden, fears that the Hangman has returned to Earth to kill him and the others, so he has hired Don Walsh's detective agency to provide him with several body-guards and to hunt down and destroy the machine. The remaining two teachers, Leila Thackery, a psychiatrist, and David Fentris, a cybernetics expert, do not share the Senator's fears.

Nemo begins by interviewing the teachers. He flies to St. Louis to talk to Dr. Thackery. Masquerading as a science writer, because he is afraid that disclosure of his connection with the case might inhibit her answers, he finds out that she believes that the Hangman went schizoid. She explains that the Hangman's brain had been imprinted with the personalities of four separate individuals and that it probably just could not integrate them. Nemo suggests that maybe just the opposite happened, that it coordinated the personalities of its four parents.

Leila explains that if that be the case then it would not want to kill them, and if it went schizoid, then, it would be unable to kill them. He asks if perhaps there might not be a simple, plain, old-fashioned reason for wanting to murder them, and she answers no.

Nemo then flies to Memphis to see Fentris. He finds that David has become a religious fanatic and believes that God is punishing them for creating artificial intelligence. But David has no intention of dying. He has a helmet that will alert him when the Hangman gets within range. He plans to contact it, bring it to him, and disconnect it.

Finally, Nemo flies to New Orleans to see Manny Burns' brother, only to learn that the police have caught Manny's killer, a punk robber who got caught in the act and hit Manny too hard.

Puzzled, Nemo calls his motel in St. Louis and discovers that Fentris has left a video-message for him. He rushes back to view the film. It is a recording of Fentris' last moments alive in which he indicts the Hangman, though he admits that he never saw his assailant.

Nemo tries to warn Leila Thackery, gets no answer, and goes to her apartment, only to find that she is dead of a broken neck. By her body, he finds Fentris' helmet and assumes that it was left by the Hangman.

He calls Walsh to report what has happened and is asked to come to the Senator's remote hunting lodge in Wisconsin as soon as possible. He does, hoping to beat the Hangman there. When he arrives, he finds that preparations are being made for the Senator's defense and that Brockden is confined to a wheelchair because of an advanced stage of cancer.

While they wait, he manages to goad the Senator into telling him what really happened. The Senator reveals that the four teachers had mishandled the Hangman the night before it was to be put into service. At a celebration party that night, they all got drunk and began to play with the Hangman. Each tried to outdo the other. As the evening wore on, they got more reckless. Finally, Manny, after a long stint at the controls maneuvered the Hangman into a bank several miles away and then turned the controls over to Brockden.

The Senator found himself in front of the bank's vault. Before he could maneuver the Hangman away, however, they were surprised by a guard. Brockden panicked, struck the guard too hard, and killed him.

To tell what they had done would have scrubbed the project, so they covered up the crime instead. They found out who the man was later and anonymously contributed funds to help his family. Now, Brockden believes that the Hangman has come back to take its revenge upon him.

Later that night, the Hangman arrives, and a battle is waged. All efforts fail to keep the Hangman away, and finally it throttles Nemo. When he awakes, he is in the Senator's big chair with the helmet on his head. The Hangman wants to talk to him.

In the next page or so, Zelazny deftly unravels the story. The Hangman, it turns out, killed no one. Fentris, it explains, was killed by one of Leila's mental patients, who then killed her. Leila had sent the man for David's helmet. Things begin to click into place for Nemo. He remembers seeing such a man coming out of a therapy session as he was on his way in to see her the first time. He later remembers seeing the same man at the airport in Memphis.

The Hangman had merely been trying to see its parents again. It says, *"I came to say good-bye to my parents. I hoped to remove any guilt they might still feel toward me concerning the days of my childhood. I wanted to show them I had recovered. I wanted to see them again"* (NL., p. 211).

Ironically, the teachers were victims of their own guilt, the very guilt that the Hangman had come to remove. Guilt is the theme of the story. The Hangman perhaps has the clearest perception of it, which he expresses in the following passage.

> *Guilt has driven and damned the race of man since the days of its earliest rationality. I am convinced that it rides with all of us to our graves. I am a product of guilt—I see that you know that. Its product, its subject, once its slave . . . But I have come to terms with it, realizing that it is a necessary adjunct of my own measure of humanity* (NL., p. 210)

A moment later the Hangman continues.

> *. . . and I see in your conclusions on many other things as well: what a stupid, perverse, shortsighted, selfish race we are. While in many ways this is true, it is but another part of the thing that guilt represents. Without guilt man would be no better than the other inhabitants of this planet—excepting certain cetaceans . . .*
> *Man, despite his enormous shortcomings, is nevertheless possessed of a greater number of kindly impulses than all the other beings where instincts are the larger part of life. These impulses, I believe, are owed directly to this capacity for guilt. It is involved in both the worst and the best of man* (NL., p. 211).

How ironic that such a profound observation comes from a machine, but perhaps it can only come from a machine, someone or something that is alienated from society, something non-human. It is clear that he believes that guilt is indigenous to man.

The Hangman will go and hang among the stars and report back to its people what it finds. It has been humanized; yet, it feels alienated because it is different. It is no coincidence that the Hangman feels a great sympathy with Nemo, because both of them are alienated from their race.

In its treatment of technology, "Home is the Hangman" is the antithesis of "The Eve of RUMOKO." Together, the two stories may be looked on as dramatic representations of those points of view expressed respectively by McHale and Schwartz. The Hangman is a disaster that turns into a success. Like the laser, it is a device whose applications lag far behind its conception. Ultimately, the Hangman is an example of how man—even with his bumbling, greed, often limited perception, brashness, immaturity, and lack of wisdom—somehow manages to extend himself.

In a small way, the story explores the question that has been asked repeatedly since the advent of the atomic age, whether man will get wise enough fast enough to prevent himself from destroying the race itself. Zelazny does not answer that question here, but in his positive presentation of the Hangman, he sheds a ray of hope.

1. Roger Zelazny, "Unpublished Letter," August 13, 1973.
2. Terry Carr, ed., "Introduction," in *An Exaltation of Stars* (New York: Simon and Schuster, 1973), p. viii.

IX.

THE AMBER NOVELS

With the publication of *The Courts of Chaos* (1978), Zelazny brings his "Amber" series to a startling conclusion. The fifth of the novels not only unravels the mutual fates of Corwin, a prince of Amber, and his kingdom but secures for its author a permanent place among the great fantasy writers. There is no question but what the series will quickly be recognized as a classic.

This is not to imply that Zelazny is new to fantasy or vice versa. Many of his early short stories were outright "sword and sorcery," especially those dealing with a character named Colonel Dilvish. (1) *Jack of Shadows* is clearly in the field, and many other Zelazny works verge on it.

"Amber" is not only a fantasy, it is a concerted and ambitious effort which creates sympathetic characters, reflects a world vividly imaginative, and weaves a plot that when unraveled produces shock after shock as it spins the reader around. Moreover, it presents an excellent picture of inter-personal relationships that are all too human.

This is not to say that the series is perfect. On the contrary, it suffers from many faults. It is often repetitious. Some of this obviously derives from the fact that it is broken up into five separate novels: *Nine Princes in Amber, The Guns of Avalon, The Sign of the Unicorn, The Hand of Oberon,* and *The Courts of Chaos.* This kind of format requires a great deal of recapitulation to maintain some sort of continuity, but sometimes it also tends to be wearying.

Moreover, some of the characters never quite come alive. Deidre never displays those qualities which Corwin finds so attractive in her, and it is often difficult to keep Flora and Fiona straight. By contrast, Dara, Benedict's daughter by the Hellmaid, Lintra; Dworkin, the mad grandfather of the clan; Brand, the power-crazy half brother; and Lorraine, Corwin's fated consort in Avalon, are beautifully drawn. And Vialle, the blind sculptress who becomes Random's Queen, is superb.

There is another fault in the novels. Some of the elements included in the world that Zelazny has cast for his story, though they are not violations of that world, are sometimes not up to the same quality as comparable elements. For example, the two oversized Siamese cats that Corwin slays at the beginning of *The Guns of Avalon* seem benign beside the manticora; the hellmaids; the Storm Hounds of Arden, whose teeth will tear metal; and Morgenstern, the terrifying horse that Julian created from shadow. Even though all things are possible in the worlds between Amber and Chaos, the cats are not as imaginative as some of the other constructions.

These difficulties are minor, however, when placed next to Amber's successes. In addition to relating a story which is fascinating and thoroughly enjoyable, the novels also make a significant statement about the human condition. Through the twistings and turnings of the plot, we watch Corwin change under the impact of his experience. When it is over, we feel his bone-weary fatigue and understand the deep wisdom he has won. Between the loss and bewilderment he feels when he sets out on his search for identity on Shadow Earth and his genuine acceptance of Random as his King near the end of *The Courts of Chaos*, Corwin achieves a nobility which makes him truly memorable.

Zelazny accomplishes the objectives he sets for the series so well because he writes from a philosophical position that is well-conceived and from a sensitivity to people which is firmly based in his own experience. In addition to its statement about the human condition, the quintet is in itself a metaphor for his own form and chaos philosophy. Nowhere else in his writing, even in *Lord of Light*, are these ideas spelled out more clearly or in such detail.

Within that metaphor, however, there is a tale, and that tale is patterned after the protype Grail-quest identified so well in Jessie L. Weston's study, *From Ritual to Romance*, a major source of Zelazny's literary conceptions.

The clues are there, occurring and recurring. Many of them fall in *The Guns of Avalon*. Early in that book, for example, Corwin comes across a knight named Lancelot du Lac, who is bleeding from a wound in the side and resting against the trunk of an oak. Dead, about him on the ground, are six other knights that he has slain. Lancelot du Lac is obviously Arthurian, and the scene is straight out of the Tristam legend. Further, the name of the former king is "Uther," echoing Uther Pendragon, Arthur's father. There are the black and white doves, to which Corwin attached notes to Eric, but which show up in Avalon. They echo the black and white sails which are present in many of the Tristam stories. Finally, there is the inescapable clue contained in the name of the kingdom itself, Avalon. That is the name of the western isle where the fatally-wounded Arthur was taken and where it was expected that he would be healed so that he might one day return to his people. There are other clues, too, but those just mentioned establish the connection with the Arthurian material beyond a doubt.

Weston's abstracted Grail-quest motifs are present in the quintet also. The first of these is the task of the hero. Abstracting from the various versions about Perceval, Gawain, and Galahad, she determines that it is the restoration of the Waste Land. The land becomes waste because the forces of its ruler have become weakened or been destroyed because of wounds, sickness, old age, or death. (2)

This certainly is the case in the quintet. Oberon is King but believed dead by almost everyone. Though he actually does live, he has been imprisoned in Chaos, so far distant from Amber that his powers have no effect. With his absence, the Black Road appears as well as the nightmare creatures from Chaos. Ironically, it is Oberon's own "Grail-quest" which provides the opportunity for his capture. He was lured away from Amber by his son Brand's story about a magical tool which could allegedly restore the damage to the Pattern, the source for all form. It is clear, however, that despite Corwin's belief that his curse had caused the blot in Amber, it is related to Oberon's loss of powers.

To complete the analogy, the hero's task must be to restore the wasted land. This is the case in the novels. Even though he does not realize it initially, Corwin's task becomes exactly that.

Corwin's initial motives are revenge and the throne. Once he realizes who he is, his love for Amber pits him against Eric. After he escapes from the cell in the palace where he has been imprisoned and finds that the Vale of Garnath has become a black and twisted wood, he vows to restore the damage to the land which he believes was caused by his curse. In the end, he is not only responsible for saving the universe from complete Chaos but has inscribed a new pattern as well, one which is different from the first and which, he thinks, has created a whole new universe.

The second Grail-legend motif that Weston identifies is that which she calls the "freeing of the waters." Literally, it is the bringing of rain to drought-stricken land or the undamming of blocked rivers. (3) Water is, of course, necessary to restoring the land's fertility.

There is such a water-freeing incident in the quintet. It occurs at the end of *The Guns of Avalon*. The forces of Chaos have invaded Amber and are attempting to overthrow it. Eric is using the Jewel of Judgment to control the weather, producing lightning and thunder with it which he is directing at the invaders. When Corwin blunders into the tempest created, he finds a strange atmosphere—a storm without rain. The imagery of the scene recalls a section of T. S. Eliot's *The Waste Land*, which was also based upon Weston's book.

Corwin must make a decision. Should he sit back and let things go as they will, or should he use the guns that he has brought with him to guarantee Amber's victory? It must be remembered that until Corwin found a gunpowder that would fire in Amber, no rifles or cannons could be used. His love of Amber overcomes his hate of Eric. He uses the guns, the battle ends with the forces of Chaos driven off, and Eric dies of his wounds. Then it begins to rain.

Rain is a symbol of purgation as well as of fertility. That it falls at this point in the story is significant. It confirms the role that Corwin has played in saving the kingdom and in "freeing the waters."

That he is responsible is reinforced by yet another parallel with the prototype legend. Weston indicates that part of the "water freeing" process is a ritual marriage which precedes it and which ensures fertility. She also indicates that in two versions of the story the hero is tempted by a fiend who appears to him " . . . in the form of a fair maiden." (4)

Corwin's affair with Dara certainly fits these characteristics. Though they do not actually marry, Oberon has marked her to be Corwin's Queen when he takes the throne, so the intention or betrothal of marriage is there. Their affair is fertile, producing Merlin, although Dara is a fiend in the form of a fair maiden. As a child of Chaos, she has shapeshifting abilities and appears in the novels on at least two occasions as something other than human.

The third motif that Weston discusses is the symbols which have attached themselves to the legend. The Grail, itself—whether in the form of cup or dish, the sword, the lance, and the stone—she concludes are life or fertility symbols of great antiquity. (5) Further, they continue to exist today as a related group as the four suits of the Tarot. The Cup (Chalice or Goblet) equals Hearts, the Lance (Wand or Scepter) equals Diamonds, the Sword equals Spades, and the Dish (Circle or Pentangles) equals Clubs. (6) Their original use, she believes, was not to forecast the future in general but rather to predict the rise and fall of the waters which brought fertility to the land. (7)

Zelazny has obviously taken over the symbols in the Tarot form. No one can read the Amber novels for long without being struck by the Tarot influence. The Trumps are obviously patterned after the twenty-two cards of the Major Arcana, which represent, as Eden Gray indicates, the distinct principles, laws, powers, or elements of Nature. Moreover, Gray feels that they are drawn from the "collective unconscious." (8) Thus, they are parallel to Jung's archetypes and perfect for Zelazny's story because it explores among other things various aspects of Corwin's experience as he grows to maturity.

There is even an historical basis for how Zelazny has adapted the cards to the novels. Gray indicates that:

> The design for each card had to be drawn anew and colored by hand. Therefore the cards became the playthings of the nobles, who could afford to assign an artist to paint their individual sets. Often the aristocracy had the Court cards drawn to resemble members of their own family or court. (9)

Zelazny does not attempt to parallel all twenty-two cards, but there is evidence to indicate that some of the characters do find their genesis in the Major Arcana. Dworkin, for example, is probably based on a card called "The Magician," Oberon on "The Emperor," Gerard on "Strength," Brand on "The Devil," and Corwin on "The Fool."

There are several parallels between Corwin and "The Fool." Corwin is the protagonist of the story and the Fool is, according to Gray, the most important card in the whole Tarot pack. (10) Though often drawn as the court jester, his image contradicts his inner meaning. A. E. Waite describes him as, " . . . a prince of the other world on his travels through this one. . . . He is the spirit in search of experience." (11) Both Corwin and the Fool begin their journeys as naive or inexperienced. In fact, Corwin has lost his memory. Both have the rose as their symbols. There is a mountain in the background of the Fool's card, and Corwin has Kolvir to defend, the mountain upon which Amber stands. Finally, both must make a journey through life, accumulating experience, and choosing between good and evil. Further evidence is added by the fact that Corwin is directly identified with the fool or its equivalent on several occasions. He makes such an identification himself near the end of *The Courts of*

Chaos, when he replies to Fiona's request that he leave the field of battle by saying, " 'I am not going with you. Leave me here. I am only *the Joker* anyway" (CC, p. 162—Emphasis mine).

Other cards of the Major Arcana appear in different ways. The "Hanged Man" card, for example, appears on a couple of occasions. The first is when Corwin and Ganelon find a youth, whose hands were tied, hanging upside down from the bough of an oak tree by his right ankle in *The Guns of Avalon*. A second appearance occurs in *The Courts of Chaos* as Corwin is making his way through a "place of bright nothingness" and sees "A man nailed to a wall, upside-down . . . " (CC, p. 78).

In the Tarot, the "Hanged Man" card signals the overcoming of the personality and the transmutation of the lower passions. (12) In other words, it corresponds to Zelazny's concept of personality metamorphosis or the maturation of his characters. As the Fool meets the Hanged Man in the Tarot, he surrenders himself to spirit and sacrifices his small desires for the greater one. (13) In the quintet, the Hanged Man symbol signals Corwin's maturation.

Certainly, the Tarot cards of the quintet fulfill the fertility role that Weston suggests is fulfilled by the four major symbols attached to the Grail legend. Amber's characters themselves are the Tarot cards in a broad way since each one is represented on the cards, and their basic purpose in the novel, with the exception of Brand, becomes the restoration of not only the land but the universe itself. Surely, this goes far beyond fertility. The Pattern governs all of the creative and forming processes in their universe.

The fourth Grail-legend motif that Weston identifies is the "Sword Dance." It is defined as a solemn, ceremonial dance, performed at stated seasons of the year, and directly and intimately connected with the ritual designed to preserve and promote the regular and ordered sequence of the processes of nature. (14) Moreover, the dance is often performed with real swords or other weapons, (15) and it often serves a second function—that of initiation (16).

There is no doubt that the action of tracing the Pattern in the quintet is equivalent to the Sword Dance. It fulfills the requirements very well. First, a dance is by definition a pattern, an observation so obvious that it could easily be missed. Second, the tracing of the Pattern not only preserves and promotes the regular processes of Nature, it establishes the very basis for them. Third, it is performed on at least one occasion with a sword, that being when Corwin uses Grayswandir to help him through the damaged Pattern areas. Fourth, it has as its object not only the preservation of the community but its very salvation as well, a characteristic not mentioned earlier here but identified by Weston. That Pattern-tracing is a restoration process is further supported by the fact that it is necessary for Corwin to retrace the Pattern to restore his memory.

Further, there is evidence to suggest that Pattern-walking is also an act of initiation. Moire, Queen of Remba, makes a comment to that effect when Deidre asks her for permission for Corwin to walk the reflection of the Pattern in her undersea kingdom. She says, "Only a son or daughter of Amber's late liege may walk this Pattern and live; and it gives to such a person a power over Shadow" (NP, p. 84). But an even more telling comment is made by Oberon to Corwin about the growth of one's powers. "You grow in strength slowly, beginning with your *initiation* into the Pattern" (CC, p. 29—Emphasis mine).

Since the act of Pattern-walking is both an act of restoration and an initiation, the two functions identified by Weston for the Sword Dance, no other conclusion can be drawn except that the two are synonymous.

Yet another motif that Weston isolates as part of the Grail-prototype is that of "The Medicine Man." Though she finds no doctor in the Grail stories and only Gawain, among the heroes, with a reputation as a healer, she believes that in an earlier tradition the hero did cure the King by means of a healing herb. (17) Further, she believes that the roles of doctor and hero did combine in certain stories and that finally the "Medicine Man" gave way to the Redeemer because the relationship between body and soul became of such importance to the drama itself. (18)

The "Medicine Man" counterpart in the Amber series is Corwin. His role as restorer has already been discussed, but it is sufficient here to state that he does, in fact, redeem form in the universe by attuning Random to the Jewel. Saving the existing state of things is, of course, a healing act.

Corwin-as-Medicine Man is reinforced by an early scene in *The Guns of Avalon*, when he saves the life of Lancelot du Lac by first treating the wound in his side and then carrying him to the Keep of Ganelon/Oberon. Corwin's role as healer is further reinforced by his association with the black and white doves, for the dove, as Weston reports, is "the badge of the Grail Knights." (19)

Though no emphasis is given to Corwin specifically as a doctor, and though he does not himself free Ganelon/Oberon, who is a loose approximation of the "Fisher King," his entire task eventually becomes the redeeming of the Pattern, which is the basis for all form, creativity, and fertility. Thus, in this sense, he well fulfills Weston's requirements for "Medicine Man."

The final motif of the prototype Grail legend is that of the "Perilous Chapel/Perilous Cemetery." Weston explains that in many versions of the Grail stories, the hero or heroine meets with a terrifying adventure in a chapel or cemetery which poses some threat to life. Though the details of this encounter vary, they often include a dead body on an altar, a black hand, strange and threatening voices, and the impression that supernatural or evil forces are at work. In one version, involving Gawain, there is a mysterious and terrible storm. In the Maneisser version of the Perceval story, there is an actual confrontation with the devil and a strange cemetery belonging to Queen Bragemore. In the cemetery are tombs with the names of the knights on them who have been slain by the Black Hand. Every day a new tomb appears with the name of the victim on it who will be killed. (20)

Zelazny's handling of this motif is quite imaginative. Rather than focusing all of the elements which make up the "Perilous Chapel" sequence in a specific location, he scatters them throughout the last half of the series. Corwin qualifies as a Grail hero by virtue of his encounter with many of the elements which make up the sequence.

Like Gawain, he encounters a terrible storm on his journey. It obliterates all form as it sweeps towards Chaos. He encounters a dead body when he witnesses Oberon's funeral procession. He encounters a black hand when, in trying to escape from Dworkin who is changing back to his monster form, he "trumps" to Chaos. Moreover, the hand of Oberon, he discovers has been manipulating him from the time he made his escape from the lighthouse at Cabra in an effort to test his worth as a successor. His confrontation with Brand during his trip to deliver the Jewel of Judgment is a metaphorical encounter with the Devil, and there is no question but what the forces of both evil and chaos are at work all about him.

The mass of evidence is overwhelming. The Grail legend prototype has given structure and dimension to Zelazny's novels. Their motifs, though modified considerably in some cases, are very much in evidence throughout the series.

As mentioned in the beginning of this section, the Amber novels represent Zelazny's simplest and clearest statement of his form and chaos philosophy. Reduced to its simplest form, the primal Pattern represents all of the creative forces in the universe and Chaos represents all of its destructive forces. The philosophy itself is discussed in great detail in other parts of this book and will not be reiterated here. Certain aspects of it, however, merit pointing out because of their relationship to good and evil.

First, form and chaos themselves exist without any moral value. They are simply two opposed forces of the universe which are constantly present to create change. Either of them can be good or bad, depending upon the circumstances and the point of view. Second, good and evil are human values and a matter of judgment. Third, form and chaos are dependent upon one another. Chaos produces the raw materials for form to create, and form produces the things that chaos destroys to provide the raw materials for new creations. Fourth, in any particular location or at any particular point in time, one or the other of these forces will be dominant. Stasis, or a balance between the two, is the one intolerable condition. Fifth, the interaction between the two forces produces a circular motion, but if form is overwhelmed by chaos and chaos is later overwhelmed by form, the second reformation is different from the first. Sixth, humans, or other creatures with intelligence, can influence the time and direction of the process. This is accomplished through will power and discipline. In the Amber novels, Dworkin tells Corwin that though both he and Oberon came from Chaos originally, they created form out of chaos by will and discipline. Finally, form and chaos are reflected in all living things. The shapeshifting abilities of Dara, Dworkin, and others display their dual natures quite dramatically, and even Corwin admits that his hands are not clean.

In the Amber quintet, good and evil are primarily represented by the symbols of the unicorn and Brand. Though the evolution of the meaning of the unicorn is strange and complicated, it is sufficient to note that it eventually came to be associated with Christ and good. (21) That it is meant to be interpreted so in the novels is indicated by the fact that Zelazny's description of it is basically identical to that which became associated with Christianity, (22) and which we all recognize: a pure white animal, smaller than a horse, with a goat's beard, cloven hooves, and a spiralled horn.

There is additional evidence to support the contention that Amber's unicorn is suggestive of Christ. Two of its characteristics, water-conning and snake-eating, imply the role of battling evil. Water-conning is the characteristic of dipping its horn into poisoned water to purify it so that the other animals can drink. (23) And its capability to eat snakes certainly suggests good battling evil since the snake is a devil symbol in Christianity. Moreover, this relationship echoes that found on the "Wheel of Fortune" Tarot card, which is drawn with Typhon, the Egyptian God of Evil, in the form of a serpent on one side and Hermes-Anubis, representing good and intelligence on the other. (24)

Another characteristic of the unicorn, found in a number of legends, is that it has a precious stone, usually a ruby, growing at the base of its horn. In one legend, there is a specific reference to the unicorn's ruby being used as one of the medicines used to cure the wound of an ailing "King of the Grail." (25)

The similarity between that legend and the appearance of the unicorn wearing the Jewel of Judgment, which is associated with red, the color of the ruby, at the end of *The Courts of Chaos* is unmistakable. Moreover, when she delivers it to Random, she has figuratively healed the wound of the "Living King."

More general evidence is found in the prototype Grail quest which runs through the quintet, which is Christ-related by definition, and in the reference to Corwin as Archangel Corwin by the dark stranger he encounters in the cave where he sought refuge from the storm on his way to Chaos. The allusion is undoubtedly to the Archangel Michael, who is known for having repelled Lucifer in Revelations with a band of loyal angels. Finally, there is the fact that Corwin is wounded in the side, as is Lancelot du Lac in *The Guns of Avalon*. This mimics Christ's wounding at Calvary.

Zelazny is not attempting to make Corwin parallel to Christ in the quintet, but rather to suggest that he is an agent of good. The imagery, allusions, and symbols are suggestive rather than specific.

The presence of evil in the novels is focused through Brand. Several clues lead to this conclusion. He is described as having flaming red hair, and the word "brand" implies fire. The imagery is traditional Devil imagery. He is an agent of Chaos, and he tempts Corwin in the final book by promising to share power with him in his reconstructed universe. This encounter, furthermore, is quite similar to that between the Fool and the

Devil in the Tarot. Gray writes, the Fool "has been shown all the secrets of life and how to use them, yet is tempted by the Devil . . . to use his newfound power to create a life of selfish gain and material pleasure." (26) It should be noted that Corwin had just learned to use the Jewel of Judgment, the universe's most powerful creative tool. This is similar to the Fool's knowledge of the secrets of life.

There is other evidence too. Brand has devilish qualities. He wants to overthrow the existing order, for example, like Lucifer, and he is a rebel. Moreover, he is associated with flashing red light (when he uses the Jewel) which mimics fire, and he is killed by a silver-tipped arrow made especially for that purpose.

The power of silver over the supernatural is well-known, especially in terms of the werewolf legends. Such is the power of silver in the quintet. Ganelon's comments from an early scene in *The Guns of Avalon* as to how the dark circle began illustrate this quality.

> And the Circle continued to widen, spreading like the ripple from a rock cast into a pond. More and more people remained, living within it . . . They began to leave the Circle in bands, marauding. They slew wantonly. They committed many atrocities and defiled places of worship. They put things to the torch when they left them. *They never stole objects of silver* (GA, p. 33—Emphasis mine).

It should also be remembered that one of Corwin's colors is silver and that his emblem is a silver rose, which in itself is a very complicated symbol because it combines the qualities of silver with those of the rose. The power of the silver rose is well-known in Chaos. In an interesting scene immediately succeeding his creation of a totally new Pattern and just after he trumps from it to Chaos, he encounters a horned rider on a great black horse whom he kills quite easily. The rider seems startled and his only comment before dying is "That rose. . . . " He refers to a wilted rose on the collar of his cloak. It is silver.

There is also a great deal of evidence of a more general nature to support the concept of Hell and the Devil. Setting a scene in Avernus, which Zelazny does in *Nine Princes in Amber* and which is the Roman name for Hell, establishes the presence of active evil in the reader's mind. This is a technique which achieves its effectiveness by quantity, so there should be many similar references scattered throughout the novels. There are, and most of them are echoes of devils. Some are, however, very specific, such as that of Strygalldwir in *The Guns of Avalon*, who is referred to as "the Horned One himself" and "the goat-man," both traditional devil terms.

There is no question but what Zelazny has cast for his readers an old-fashioned psychomachia. He supports these concepts by gathering images and symbols relevant to each about the unicorn and Brand.

As stated earlier in this chapter, one of the objectives that the Amber quintet sets for itself is to make a statement about the human condition. This it accomplishes quite nicely through Corwin, posing and answering the standard questions: "what is the purpose of man," "what is his relationship to other men," and "what is his relationship to the universe."

The questions are posed through Corwin's desires, motives, actions, thoughts, and situations, and they are answered by the state of his personality at the end of the series. Not too surprisingly, the answers are rather basic. They can be summarized in several positive statements.

First, it is possible for man to change considerably under the impact of his experience. In fact, the change may be of such a degree as to be described as metamorphic. This is a theme which runs through much of Zelazny's writing and which Joe Sanders calls "Zelazny's great theme" (28).

This capacity for unlimited growth is dramatically presented in the development of Corwin and supported by the concurrent development of Random. It can best be seen by comparing what Corwin is at the beginning of the series with what he has become at its end. When we first see him, he is primarily motivated by his hate for Eric, his desire to avenge himself, and his quest for his memory. Shortly thereafter, he wants the throne of Amber, but it is as much to keep Eric from claiming it as it is to claim it for himself. This indicates that revenge is still foremost in his mind. Further, he distrusts most of his family, even Random, and he respects his father out of fear rather than love.

By the end of the series, he has learned the value of love, respect, sacrifice, and family. He has gained a deep understanding of self, and he has developed genuine wisdom.

Several remarks in the novels support Corwin's change in personality, and the rose symbol marks its degree. The rose is usually a symbol of transformation in Zelazny's writing. It is not an accident, for example, that just prior to his inscription of a new Pattern, he picks up a rose cast toward him by the auburn-haired spirit of Time, nor that the same rose is a physical cue for his inscription of the Pattern later. It is likewise a symbol of his own transformation and of his capability to transform, for it is his emblem.

Second, man must seek out experience if he is to fulfill his potential. This concept is presented in the continuing dialogue between Corwin and Hugi, a bird of ill-omen, as they journey towards Chaos, but it is perhaps stated most succinctly in Corwin's final comments just prior to twisting off Hugi's head. In explaining why he continues to push onward even though the storm is very near, he says, " 'If I fail here, it will become Absolute. As for me, I must try, for as long as there is a breath within me, to raise up a Pattern against it. I do this because I am what I am, and I am the man who could have been king in Amber' " (CC, p. 114). In an earlier exchange, Corwin says that if a person is going to make the trip through life he may as well make it worthwhile.

Third, it is not only achieving the goal that is important but the style with which it is accomplished. Corwin expresses this concept as he inscribes the new Pattern. He knows that the universe he is creating will be an extension of himself when it is finished just as the existing Pattern is itself an extension of Dworkin's mind. He knows that the richness of the new universe, its character so to speak, will be determined by the details that he puts into the new Pattern, so he chooses something that he remembers with affection to transcribe into the basic form, Paris of 1905. Remembering the richness of the place and the mood of the time, he says, " 'I had forgotten . . . The details. . . . The touches that make for life' " (CC, p. 118).

The fourth and final statement about man is that he must ultimately be pragmatic. Though ideals provide excellent targets for him to aim at, they are not realistic. To survive, a man must do whatever a particular situation calls for.

This attitude is best shown as Corwin's encounter with Lord Borel, Dara's old fencing master, when they finally meet on the battlefield at Chaos. Borel expects Corwin to be chivalric. He even removes his breast armor so that their fight will be fair.

Corwin, weary from inscribing the new Pattern, is struck by the stupidity and presumptuousness of Borel's actions. Battle is not a game to him. So, Corwin tricks Borel and then kills him by throwing a cloak over his head, kicking him from his horse, and skewering him when he is down. This act turns Dara against him, but when she charges Corwin with being dishonorable, he does not even reply to her. He accepts the consequences of his actions and knows that it would be useless to try to change her impression of the encounter.

These four principles, then, summarize man's purpose in life and give an impression of its quality. To get at man's relationship to other men, we must examine Corwin's relationship to other members of his family.

When the story begins, Corwin trusts no one in the family, but then neither do any of the others, even the patriarch Oberon. It must be remembered that most of the events of the plot develop out of the relationship of the family members. It is because he assumes that Corwin and Brand are working together to overthrow Amber that Caine sneaks into Corwin's room and stabs him, for example. It is significant that he does not bother to get hard evidence that Corwin is involved before he acts. Oberon's betrayal of Brand, Corwin's amnesia, the grouping of the family into two throne-seeking triads, all are the product of the mutual distrust, misunderstandings, and suspicions that exists among family members. This is how men often relate to one another, Zelazny believes, but this is not necessarily how it is supposed to be.

That is shown in the final relationship between the brothers and sisters. They accept Random as their King. They believe, trust, and love one another. Most of all, they have learned to respect one another.

Finally, how man should relate to the universe at large is best seen in the peace that Corwin finds by the end of the story. Both Corwin and Zelazny believe that though man is buffeted by the forces of form and chaos, he may find peace within when he makes peace without. This comes when he learns to live in concert with those forces.

1. Lin Carter, *Imaginary Worlds* (New York: Ballantine Books, 1973), p. 154.
2. Jessie L. Weston, *From Ritual to Romance* (Garden City, NY: Doubleday and Company, 1957), p. 23.
3. Ibid., p. 26.

4. Ibid., p. 32.
5. Ibid., p. 66.
6. Ibid., p. 77.
7. Ibid., p. 80.
8. Eden Gray, *A Complete Guide to the Tarot* (New York: Crown Publishers, 1970), p. 20.
9. Ibid., p. 10.
10. Ibid., p. 149.
11. Ibid.
12. Ibid., p. 34.
13. Ibid., p. 150.
14. Weston, p. 81.
15. Ibid., p. 85.
16. Ibid., p. 89.
17. Weston, p. 108.
18. Ibid., pp. 109-110.
19. Ibid., p. 134.
20. Ibid., p. 177.
21. Odell Shepard, *The Lore of the Unicorn* (New York: Barnes and Noble, 1967), p. 81.
22. Ibid., p. 71.
23. Ibid., pp. 150-154.
24. Gray, p. 32.
25. Shepard, p. 82.
26. Gray, p. 150.
27. Joseph Sanders, "Zelazny: Unfinished Business," in *Voices for the Future*, ed. Thomas D. Clareson (Bowling Green, OH: Bowling Green University Popular Press, 1978), II, 15.

X.

... AND OTHER STORIES

In a work as limited as this, it is impossible to discuss all of those pieces of Zelazny's fiction which are worthy of reading. Such novels as *Damnation Alley, Isle of the Dead,* and *Doorways in the Sand,* and other shorter works such as "This Mortal Mountain," "This Moment of the Storm," "The Keys to December," "The Man Who Loved the Faioli," and "The Engine at Heartspring's Center" should not necessarily be thought of as inferior to the Hugo and Nebula Award winners just because they did not, themselves, win one of those awards. Many fan-favorites are, in fact, included in the group mentioned above. Each of them has qualities which make its reading well worth the effort.

Damnation Alley, while not a story of great substance, is nonetheless important because it is the first of Zelazny's novels to be made into a movie. Unfortunately, it was badly handled.

The story, almost all action, is set after an atomic war which has left the United States devastated. Only two pockets of civilization remain: one in Boston and the other in Los Angeles. Between them is the "Alley," an irradiated area, cruel and violent, full of dangerous plant and animal mutations and fraught with geologic and atmospheric disturbances. When Boston is beset with bubonic plague, Hell Tanner, the novel's main character and the last living member of the Hell's Angels motorcycle gang, is drawn reluctantly into running the "Alley" with a serum which will save Boston. The rest of the plot is his journey.

The theme of the novel is the interdependence of man. It is developed by displaying the alternative to technology which is untempered by humanism. That alternative is alienation. It shows up in the character of Hell, who is a rebel and in the symbols of Boston, Los Angeles, and the "Alley." Boston is, in fact, doubly isolated, being cut off from the only other major pocket of civilization and its citizens being deprived from human contact by the nature of the plague itself. The "Alley," with its many terrors, dramatizes the effects produced by a society which denies man the opportunity to develop his potential, to engage in deep and meaningful relationships, and to maintain his integrity. Ironically, it was created by man himself. At another level, it represents God's justice for men who have turned away from basic Christian precepts.

The Noh Play, another major symbol, focuses the character of Hell Tanner, expands and supports the interdependence of man theme and raises the general level of the novel. Though it has been modified to fit the needs of the story and to make it more understandable to a western audience, it represents the society that Zelazny wishes could exist, one that stresses the beautiful, the ideal, the humane, and the individual.

Isle of the Dead, one of Zelazny's most popular novels and winner of the French Prize, the *Prix Apollo* in 1972, is squarely in the mold of

Zelazny's early work. It is highly mythic; its themes are revenge, greed, power, and immortality; its characterization is handled in a fashion similar to that of *This Immortal*, *The Dream Master*, and *Lord of Light*; and its conceptual basis lies in the form and chaos philosophy. One of the significant differences is that here Zelazny has constructed his own mythology for the story rather than drawing heavily from an existing one.

The story is about Francis Sandow, a virtual immortal, one of the galaxy's richest men, and a worldscaper. Worldscaping is an ancient art of the Pei'ans, an alien race, which has learned the secret of how to draw on the hidden powers of the universe to create, modify, and destroy worlds. The power is based in their religion and focused through their gods.

The story begins when Sandow receives a note which makes him believe that six dead persons—some friends, some enemies—are once again alive. One of them is his former wife, Kathy. The note is accompanied by pictures of Kathy and one of Sandow's girlfriends, Ruth. It is signed by someone named Green Green and directs him to a planet he had created, Isle of the Dead. Moreover, it bears the ideogram for Belion, the Pei'an fire god who lives under the earth.

Sandow eventually identifies Green Green as a Pei'an named Gringrintharl of the city of Delpei, who had failed his own planet shaper test and bore a grudge against Sandow because Sandow is an outsider.

Events finally bring Sandow to the Isle of the Dead, where he finds that the order of things has been changed. A confrontation with Green Green reveals that the Pei'an had, in fact, stolen the personality tapes so that he could revenge himself on Sandow, but that one of those he had recalled was Mike Shandon, an agent that Sandow had killed years earlier in hand to hand combat. Shandon had become Green Green's protege, but once when the Pei'an had called Belion to him, Mike made a deal with him and Belion switched his allegiance to Shandon.

Sandow blackmails the hurt Green Green into helping him. There is an inevitable confrontation between Shandon/Belion and Sandow/Shimbo. Shimbo of Darktree, Shrugger of Thunders, is the god whose name Sandow has taken and who is the ancient enemy of Belion.

Sandow eventually destroys Shandon and faces down Belion, but he learns that the gods are real, that contrary to his earlier belief that confirmation as a Name was only a psychological device to coordinate the talents of the subconscious, the ritual did, in fact, put the name-bearer into contact with the real gods and the secret power of the universe.

Sandow, as so many of Zelazny's characters, is a symbol of form, and Shandon/Belion is a symbol of chaos. In this case, form is connected to good and chaos to evil. So, the ultimate result in the novel is a confrontation between good and evil.

"The Keys to December" is a beautiful and moving story about a genetically altered creature, a catform, named Jarry Dark. Highly intelligent and sensitive, Dark is one of approximately twenty-eight thousand catforms who were optioned to General Mining Incorporated to run their operation on a coldworld called Alynol. Unfortunately, before they could get there, the planet was destroyed by a nova, and they are left alienated on the other inhabitable worlds of the galaxy. They are prisoners of their physiology, breathing methane and comfortable only when the temperature reaches -50 Centigrade.

Dark is a financial genius, who helps form the December Club. The Club pools its money, which Dark soon turns into a fortune, and buys a planet and the equipment necessary to alter it so that it can accommodate them. They also buy sleep chambers where they will rest until the conversion of their climate has taken place, a period of three thousand years.

The equipment requires monitoring, however, so all catforms agree to stand watches during that period. Dark stands his with his fiancee, Sanza Barati. While awake, they watch the development of the native life-forms. During the period that passes, Dark becomes aware of his responsibility for the life-forms, particularly the bipeds, who begin to show signs of intelligence. He realizes that the catforms have altered evolutionary patterns and that they may well kill off what will become an intelligent life-form unless they slow down the climate-change.

In a particularly tragic incident, Sanza is killed while saving Jarry's life. He then blackmails the other catforms into slowing down the change process so that the bipeds, whom he has named Redforms, will have a chance. He knows that they must be monitored though, so he agrees to live out a normal lifespan rather than waiting for a new Alynol. Thus, he has learned the value of sacrifice and the responsibility of godhood.

"This Moment in the Storm" tells the story of Godfrey Holmes, a man who has chosen to alienate himself from his time and his culture by jumping from planet to planet in suspended animation in an effort to find that one place and time where he will live his "golden age," where all things come together happily for him.

He believes that he has found it on a planet named Tierra del Cygnus, Land of the Swan. He has fallen in love with Eleanor Wyeth, the Mayor of Beta, the main town on the planet. They survive a terrible storm, only to have Eleanor murdered by a looter in a senseless and absurd act after it is over.

The story is particularly interesting because it makes an attempt to portray contemporary man alienated and caught up in the absurdness of life. It is existential in this sense. Holmes is also a departure from the usual Zelazny protagonists. In linking "chaos" with the storm and Eleanor's death, the story also links the existential view of man, as put forth by Camus and others, with Zelazny's form and chaos philosophy.

"This Mortal Mountain" is another story which reflects the absurdity of life. Jack Summers, nicknamed Whitey, is the ultimate mountain climber. He conquered Everest at twenty-three and the largest known mountain in the known universe at thirty-one, Kasla, over 89,000 feet high.

Now, however, a new mountain, "The Gray Sister," presents itself on a planet named Diesel. It is forty miles high and has never been climbed. It presents the ultimate challenge to Whitey, known as Mad Jack to some because of his daring. Whitey finally assembles a group and makes the assault, only to find their efforts impeded by a series of illusions: a bird-shaping thing, a beautiful girl, an angel, and many snakes. They seem to be energy creatures of some sort, though no such life form is known.

Despite the obstacles, Whitey manages to climb "The Gray Sister." He goes on regardless of the difficulty of the climb or the illusions. When he reaches the top, he finds a cave, and in it a chamber where a girl is sleeping. The illusions, he discovers, are fear-forms projected by a computer which was programmed to protect her. Assuming that she is a prisoner, Whitey breaches the last protective device, a ring of fire, and wakes her. Ironically, he finds out that Linda, as the girl is named, was placed into cryogenic sleep because she had contracted what was, at the time, an incurable disease, Dawson's plague. The computer had tapped her mind to find fear-forms but in doing so, had also projected her great desire to be freed. This was what led Whitey to believe that she was a prisoner.

The story ends with the paradox unresolved. Linda may well have been condemned to death by the very attempt to save her. Doc, a member of the climbing party, is on his way to the chamber, but Whitey does not know if he can provide a serum for the plague. Moreover, in yet another irony, he learns that the mountain is hollow inside and that she reached the chamber by coming up in a flier. Her people had flown it repeatedly as an amusement ride. Their name for the mountain is prophetically, Purgatorio, which suggests that the story contains an analogue in Dante and that Whitey has made an ascent, rather than descent, to Hell.

Like "This Moment of the Storm," "This Mortal Mountain" expresses the existential absurdity of life. Death comes when we are least prepared for it, justice is not always fair, life is not logical. We are asked to be responsible for our actions, yet do not often understand their full implications.

"The Engine at Heartspring's Center" is a beautifully told bitter-sweet love story. It concerns a man named Charles Eliot Borkman, who several years earlier had saved the lives of several persons when a spaceliner he was traveling on got the wrong coordinates and came out of its jump through hyperspace too close to a nova. The incident was thought to be an assassination attempt and Borkman was declared a hero, but in the process of saving everyone, he lost half of his body. Bionically repaired, Borkman became virtually immortal and was nicknamed the "Bork."

At the time of the story, weary with life, he has chosen to go to a euthanasia center. Once there, however, he finds that he likes the place. Living at the end of entropy is peaceful, so he refuses to go through with his contract.

Enter then a girl named Nora, who claims to have made a mistake and does not want to go through with her contract either. Borkman meets her on the beach, running from the Center, and takes her in. He falls in love with her and she with him. Later, he discovers that she was sent from the Center to kill him.

Instead of carrying out her task as directed, however, she chooses to join him in death. She injects him with one ampule of poison and herself with another. The dosage is not sufficient to kill him, so he wakes up and finds her dying. He forgives her and they cling together as she dies.

In this story, with its classic *Romeo and Juliet* ending, we encounter once again a familiar Zelazny theme, the power of love to add meaning to life in the endless growth of any individual. At the very verge of death, Borkman learns that there are new experiences to be encountered. The environment of the euthanasia center itself is enough to sway him from going through with the contract, and Nora proves to be an adventure in her own right.

"The Man Who Loved the Faioli" is an exquisitely told story that poses love against immortality and emotion against reason: John Auden, a man dying of an incurable disease, has chosen to remain more or less alive by artificial means. He sacrifices his emotional existence, however, by this choice and becomes a prisoner of his own physical processes in a life-in-death existence. He becomes further alienated from humanity when he is assigned to be the caretaker of the universe's graveyard. His only contact is with the robots who deliver the bodies of the dead into his keeping.

Then, a fragile, legendary creature called the Faioli comes to the planet. She is the essence of female beauty and, as the legend goes, gives her love to those who are dying. Intrigued by her beauty, Auden switches off his support systems and becomes human once more. He lives with her for the month, enjoying the pleasures of her body and relishing his love for her.

When Auden tries to explain to the Faioli, named Sythia, that he does not have to die, she does not understand, but she touches the switch which once more turns on his support system. He disappears from her sight and is thus relieved of making a decision as to whether to die or to live, emotionless and alone.

As Thomas Monteleone has accurately pointed out, (1) "The Man Who Loved the Faioli" bears a great similarity to "The Keys to December" in that both protagonists are placed into a position where they may choose between a short, emotional life or a coldly logical state of near immortality. Dark chooses the former; the latter is chosen for Auden.

The story also bears similarities to "This Mortal Mountain" and "This Moment of the Storm" in its portrayal of what are the existential dichotomies of life, and it mirrors the two sides of man as Zelazny often presents them. Compare, for example, the choice of Auden with the definition of man as Sam explains him to the demon, Taraka, in *Lord of Light*.

Doorways in the Sand, one of Zelazny's latest novels, is a departure from anything that he has previously published. It is light in tone and comic in effect. The book has been well-received, being nominated for both the Hugo and Nebula, and being chosen by the American Library Association as one of 1976's Best Books for Young Adults.

The story is about Fred Cassidy, a perpetual undergraduate student, who is hooked on climbing high buildings and other places. Fred inadvertently becomes involved in a search for the missing star-stone, an alien artifact on loan to Earth. Suspected of having stolen it himself, he is forced to find it. Pursued by hoodlums, intergalactic police in disguise, and telepaths, Fred eventually finds the stone and saves Earth from galactic embarrassment.

Doorways in the Sand is Zelazny's lightest-weight, most accessible novel. It takes its form from the ever-popular espionage-suspense story and is easy reading. (2) It marks Zelazny's testing of his own "perpetual growth of the individual" theme in its departure from those models which he has already proven he can write well. (3) Moreover, it satisfies his desire to write what might loosely be labeled a children's story.

Roger Zelazny is a truly gifted writer, one who is not afraid to test his talents. Each of his stories, whether judged in the long run to be successful, brings its readers something new: an idea, a technique, an observation, a view of the human condition. This reason alone makes him worth reading.

1. Thomas F. Monteleone, "Fire and Ice—On Roger Zelazny's Short Fiction," *Algol*, 13, No. 2 (Summer 1976), 14.
2. Joseph Sanders, "Zelazny: Unfinished Business," in *Voices for the Future*, ed. Thomas D. Clareson (Bowling Green, OH: Bowling Green University Popular Press, 1978), II, 22.
3. Ibid., p. 23.

XI.

SELECTIVELY ANNOTATED
PRIMARY BIBLIOGRAPHY

A.   STORIES

1   " . . . And Call Me Conrad [I] ." *Magazine of Fantasy and Science Fiction*, October 1965, pp. 5-57.

2   " . . . And Call Me Conrad [II] ." *Magazine of Fantasy and Science Fiction*, November 1965, pp. 39-97.

3   "Angel, Dark Angel." *Galaxy*, August 1967, pp. 57-67.

4   "Auto-de-fé." In *Dangerous Visions*. Ed. Harlan Ellison. New York: Doubleday, 1967, pp. 500-507.

5   "The Bells of Shoredan." *Fantastic*, March 1966, pp. 6-21.

6   "The Borgia Hand." *Amazing*, March 1963, pp. 73-76.

7   "But Not the Herald." *Magazine of Horror*, Winter 1965, pp. 33-35.

8   "Circe Has Her Problems." *Amazing*, April 1963, pp. 70-75.

9   "Collector's Fever." *Galaxy*, June 1964, pp. 129-131.

10 "Comes Now the Power." *Magazine of Horror*, Winter 1966, pp. 55-60.

11 "Come to Me Not in Winter's White." *Magazine of Fantasy and Science Fiction*, October 1969, pp. 24-33. Written with Harlan Ellison. Carl Manos, the world's richest man, builds a room that will slow down time for his dying wife but finds that love is often motivated by loneliness.

12 "Corrida." *Anubis*, I, No. 3 (1968), 4-5. Michael Cassidy, an attorney from New York, plays an unwilling but very important role in a bull fight.

13 "Devil Car." *Galaxy*, June 1965, pp. 151-170.

14 "Dismal Light." *If*, May 1968, pp. 60-71.

15 "Divine Madness." *Magazine of Horror*, Summer 1966, pp. 30-35. A man gets a second chance with his dead wife, when he suddenly finds himself spinning backwards in time.

16 "The Doors of His Face, the Lamps of His Mouth." *Magazine of Fantasy and Science Fiction*, March 1965, pp. 4-30. Carlton Davits, a wealthy playboy, searches for the ultimate fish in the seas of Venus and, in the process, finds himself.

17 "The Engine at Heartspring's Center." *Analog*, July 1974, pp. 70-76. The Bork, a bionic creature, goes to a euthanasia center to die, decides not to, falls in love with a girl named Nora, and is deceived by her.

18 "The Eve of RUMOKO." In *Three For Tomorrow*. Ed. Terry Carr. New York: Meredith Press, 1969, pp. 85-152. The first of Zelazny's "no-name" detective stories. Nemo catches two saboteurs and permits an island-making project to go off on schedule only to find that they were right (Cf. 28, 33 below).

19 "Final Dining." *Fantastic*, February 1963, pp. 77-84.
20 "For A Breath I Tarry." *Fantastic*, September 1966, pp. 6-37. First published in *New Worlds* in March 1966, this is the correct version of the story. The text of the earlier one is inaccurate. Frost, a robot-computer, learns what it means to be a man, and then, when frozen bodies are found intact in the Arctic, he takes steps to assure that humanity will be restored to Earth.
21 "The Furies." *Amazing*, June 1965, pp. 61-91. Victor Corgo, Captain of the *Wallaby*, wages a personal war against mankind when society decides to destroy the *Drillen*, a tribe of very ugly natives who saved his life. He is pursued by three mutants, and both he and the last *Drillen* survivor are destroyed.
22 "The Game of Blood and Dust." *Galaxy*, April 1975, pp. 5-8.
23 "The Graveyard Heart." *Fantastic*, March 1964, pp. 20-71.
24 "The Great Slow Kings." *Worlds of Tomorrow*, December 1963, pp. 97-102.
25 "He That Moves." *Worlds of If*, January 1968, pp. 153-159.
26 "He Who Shapes [I]." *Amazing*, January 1965, pp. 72-113.
27 "He Who Shapes [II]." *Amazing*, February 1965, pp. 102-122.
28 "Home is the Hangman." *Analog*, November 1975, pp. 12-66. The third "no-name" detective story. Nemo is hired to protect a Senator from a unique machine but finds that it has no intention of killing the man. (Cf. numbers 18, 33.)
29 "Horseman." *Fantastic*, August 1962, pp. 109-111.
30 "Is There A Demon Lover in the House." *Heavy Metal*, September 1977, pp. 43-44.
31 "The Keys to December." *New Worlds*, August 1966, pp. 115-141. Jarry Dark, a genetically engineered mutant called a catform, learns the responsibilities of being a god and eventually sacrifices his life for those who worship him.
32 "King Solomon's Ring." *Fantastic*, October 1963, pp. 49-67.
33 " 'Kjwalll'kje'k'koothailll'kje'k." In *An Exhaltation of Stars*. Ed. Terry Carr. New York: Simon and Schuster, 1973, pp.61-130 (Cf. numbers 18, 28 above). The second of the "no-name" detective stories. Nemo is hired to clear a pack of dolphins of a homicide charge and through a telepath participates in a religious dreamsong.
34 "The Last Inn on the Road." *New Worlds*, October 1967, pp. 55-57. Written with Danny Plachta.
35 "Love is an Imaginary Number." *New Worlds*, January 1966, pp. 86-92.
36 "Lucifer." *Worlds of Tomorrow*, June 1964, pp. 81-85. A man named Carlson brings a dead city to life for ninety-three seconds because he is lonesome.
37 "The Malatesta Collection." *Fantastic*, April 1963, pp. 47-52.
38 "The Man Who Loved the Faioli." *Galaxy*, June 1967, pp. 67-73.

John Auden, an incurably ill human and caretaker of a planet where the dead of the universe are deposited, learns love from a fragile creature called a Faioli.

39 "Mine is the Kingdom." *Amazing*, August 1963, pp. 106-120. Last story Zelazny wrote under the pseudonym of Harrison Denmark.

40 "The Misfit." *Amazing*, October 1963, pp. 116-119. A man named Jackson finds his dreams to be fitful.

41 "Monologue for Two." *Fantastic*, May 1963, pp. 110-111. Written under the pseudonym of Harrison Denmark.

42 "The Monster and the Maiden." *Galaxy*, December 1964, pp. 104-105.

43 "Moonless in Byzantium." *Amazing*, December 1962, pp. 35-39.

44 "A Museum Piece." *Fantastic*, June 1963, pp. 119-127. Jay Smith, an unsuccessful artist, hides in a museum by posing as a statue. There, he meets an alien girl, who has been masquerading as a mobile.

45 "Nine Starships Waiting." *Fantastic*, March 1963, pp. 96-125.

46 "No Award." *Saturday Evening Post*, 249, No. 1 (January/February 1977, 57, 93-95. A man foils what appears to be a perfect assassination plot when he stops himself from killing the President.

47 "Of Time and the Yan." *Magazine of Fantasy and Science Fiction*, June 1965, pp. 110-112.

48 "On the Road to Splenoba." *Fantastic*, January 1963, pp. 115-122. Babakov, a member of the People's Party, makes an unfortunate overnight stop on his way to Splenoba and meets a vampire.

49 "Passage to Dilfar." *Fantastic*, February 1965, pp. 49-53.

50 "Passion Play." *Amazing*, August 1962, pp. 31-33. A robot, living at a time in the distant future long after man has disappeared, turns himself off in an act of ritual suicide and crashes his Ferrari during an auto race.

51 "A Rose for Ecclesiastes." *Magazine of Fantasy and Science Fiction*, November 1963, pp. 5-35. Gallinger, a conceited poet, saves a Martian race bent on suicide and learns humility in the process.

52 "The Salvation of Faust." *Magazine of Fantasy and Science Fiction*, July 1964, pp. 76-79.

53 "Song of the Blue Baboon." *If*, August 1968, pp. 91-94.

54 "The Stainless Steel Leech." *Amazing*, April 1963, pp. 115-118. Written under the pseudonym of Harrison Denmark.

55 "The Steel General." *Worlds of If*, January 1969, pp. 67-98, 156-158.

56 "The Teachers Rode a Wheel of Fire." *Fantastic*, October 1962, pp. 108-112.

57 "Thelinde's Song." *Fantastic*, June 1965, pp. 5-11.

58 "A Thing of Terrible Beauty." *Fantastic*, April 1963, pp. 75-80. Written under the pseudonym of Harrison Denmark.

59 "This Moment of the Storm." *Magazine of Fantasy and Science Fiction*, June 1966, pp. 4-30. Godfrey Holmes, a man alienated from the human race because of his numerous interstellar trips in suspended animation, finds his residence on the planet Cygnus is not his golden moment in time.

60 "This Mortal Mountain." *Worlds of If*, March 1967, pp. 37-67. Whitey, the ultimate mountain climber, masters a forty-mile high mountain and finds a girl sleeping inside it.

61 "Threshold of the Prophet." *Fantastic*, May 1963, pp. 67-71.

62 "The Year of the Good Seed." *Galaxy*, December 1969, pp. 85-89. Written with Danny Plachta.

B. NOVELS, COLLECTIONS, AND EDITED ANTHOLOGIES

63 *Bridge of Ashes*. New York: Signet Books, 1976. Dennis Guise, the world's greatest telepath, becomes a pawn in a battle to save the world from aliens. An idiot child throughout most of the story, his personality must be restructured so that he can serve as an example for the Dark Man, himself an alien who has been the enemy of the oppressors for centuries.

64 *The Courts of Chaos*. New York: Doubleday and Company, 1978. The last of the "Amber" novels (Cf. 72, 73, 79, 81). Corwin proceeds on a final attempt to restore order to the universe. He loses the Jewel of Judgment to Brand after he inscribes a new Pattern, but trumps (travels astrally) to Chaos in time to see Brand's destruction, Random chosen King, Oberon's funeral, and the final triumph of form. Serialized in *Galaxy*, November 1977, December 1977-January 1978, and February 1978.

65 *Creatures of Light and Darkness*. New York: Doubleday and Company, 1969. Anubis and Horus embark on separate missions to destroy once and for all the Prince Who Was A Thousand, but neither is prepared for the strange people or circumstances they meet. Exerpts published in *New Worlds*, July 1967, and *If*, November 1968 and March 1969.

66 *Damnation Alley*. New York, G. P. Putnam's, 1969. Expanded from a shorter version originally published in *Galaxy*, October 1967. Hell Tanner, last of the Hell's Angels, must take a serum from Los Angeles to Boston to save the city from a plague. To do so, he must run "Damnation Alley," an irradiated area in the center of the country created by an atomic war.

67 *Deus Irae*. New York: Harper and Row, 1976. Though Zelazny and Philip K. Dick appear as co-authors, most of the novel was written by Dick. Zelazny contributed only the ending.

68 *The Doors of His Face, the Lamps of His Mouth and Other Stories*. New York: Doubleday and Company, 1971. Collects "The Doors of His Face, the Lamps of His Mouth," "A Rose for

Ecclesiastes," "The Keys to December," "Devil Car," "The Monster and the Maiden," "Collector's Fever," "This Mortal Mountain," "This Moment of the Storm," "The Great Slow Kings," "A Museum Piece," "Divine Madness," "Corrida," "Love is an Imaginery Number," "The Man Who Loved the Faioli," and "Lucifer."

69   *Doorways in the Sand*. New York: Harper and Row, 1976. Fred Cassidy, perpetual undergraduate student and inveterate climber of high buildings, gets involved in a search for the star-stone, an alien artifact on loan to Earth. Suspected of stealing it himself, he must help find it while being pursued by hoodlums, telepaths, and strangely disguised intergalactic police. Serialized in *Analog*, June, July, and August 1975.

70   *The Dream Master*. New York: Ace Books, 1966. An expanded version of "He Who Shapes" (Cf. numbers 26 and 27). Some 10,000 words were added to "He Who Shapes" to create *The Dream Master*. Charles Render, a neuroparticipation therapist, overestimates his ability to control a patient's dreams and is drawn into her final mad fantasy.

71   *Four For Tomorrow*. New York: Ace Books, 1967. Collects four of Zelazny's best short novels: "The Furies," "The Graveyard Heart," "The Doors of His Face, the Lamps of His Mouth," and "A Rose for Ecclesiastes."

72   *The Guns of Avalon*. New York: Doubleday and Company, 1972. The second of the "Amber" novels (Cf. numbers 64, 73, 79, 81). Corwin escapes from his cell in Amber to the Shadow World of Avalon, where he meets Ganelon and Dara, a creature of Chaos, by whom he has a son named Merlin. After defeating the "Dark Circle," he creates a gunpowder which will fire in Amber and plans to overthrow his brother Eric. When he does return, however, he finds Amber being attacked by creatures from Chaos. He saves the kingdom, Eric dies in battle but wills him the Jewel of Judgment, and Dara walks the Pattern, the primal essence of Amber and of form.

73   *The Hand of Oberon*. New York: Doubleday and Company, 1976. The fourth of the "Amber" novels (Cf. numbers 64, 72, 79, 81). Corwin discovers that Ganelon is Amber's missing king, his father Oberon, and that the city is itself shadow, that is, created illusion. An attempt is made to repair the damaged, real Pattern, the Jewel of Judgment is recovered, and Brand is revealed as the traitor.

74   *Isle of the Dead*. New York: Ace Books, 1967. Francis Sandow, a virtual immortal and worldscaper, has become a god of the Pei'ans, aligning himself with the mythic god, Shimbo of Darktree. Six people who have been dead for hundreds of years suddenly reappear, and Sandow is forced to face Shimbo's ancient enemy, Belion, in a final battle for power.

75 *Jack of Shadows.* New York: Walker and Company, 1971. Jack of Shadows, a master thief who has supernatural powers over shadow, seeks vengeance on his enemies and tries to reunite the world, which now exists as two distinct kingdoms because it no longer rotates. Serialized in the *Magazine of Fantasy and Science Fiction*, July and August, 1971.

76 *Lord of Light.* New York: Doubleday and Company, 1967. Mahasamatman, an immortal, overthrows the corrupt "Deicrat" system of gods, which is modeled after the Hindu pantheon, and frees mankind to make his own decisions about his destiny. In the process, "Sam" must face Yama, the god of Death, and Kali/Brahma, his former wife. Excerpts in *Magazine of Fantasy and Science Fiction*, April and June, 1967.

77 *My Name is Legion.* New York: Ballantine Books, 1976. Collects the three "no name" detective stories: "The Eve of RUMOKO," " 'Kjwalll'kj'k'koothailll'kje'k," and "Home is the Hangman" (Cf. numbers 18, 28, 31).

78 *Nebula Awards Stories Three.* New York, 1968. Zelazny edited these award-winning stories.

79 *Nine Princes in Amber.* New York: Doubleday and Company, 1970. The first book of the "Amber" novels (Cf. numbers 64, 72, 73, 81). Corwin, the protagonist, awakes on Shadow-Earth and embarks on a search for his missing memory. Random, a brother, takes him to Amber where he meets his half-brother, Eric, who has claimed the vacant throne. After an unsuccessful attempt to overthrow Eric, Corwin's eyes are put out and he is thrown into prison. There, his eyes regenerate and he meets the mad dwarf, Dworkin, who provides him a means of escape.

80 *Poems.* Washington, D.C.: DISCON II, 1974. A collection of poems from Zelazny's works to commemorate him being Guest of Honor at DISCON II. Illustrated by Jack Gaughan.

81 *Sign of the Unicorn.* New York: Doubleday and Company, 1975. The third of the "Amber" novels (Cf. numbers 64, 72, 73, 79). Corwin reigns uneasily in Amber, though he has never officially taken the throne. Brand, another brother, is rescued from a prison near Chaos, and Corwin begins to master the powers of the Jewel of Judgment, a talisman that controls weather and has a number of unsuspected powers. Serialized in *Galaxy*, January, February, and March 1975.

82 *This Immortal.* New York: Ace Books, 1966. An expansion of " . . . And Call Me Conrad" (Cf. numbers 1, 2). Conrad Nomikos, a mutant immortal, must protect Cort Myshtigo, a Vegan, from a radical group which wishes to assassinate him, and as a result, he literally inherits the Earth, which has been devastated by an atomic war.

83   *Today We Choose Faces* New York: Signet Books, 1973. A story
      about clones. Lange, the leader of the Family, ignores a voice
      that tells him to pull pin seven, for he believes that he can
      deal with the mysterious attacker who threatens to destroy
      the Family by himself.

84   *To Die in Italbar*. New York: Doubleday and Company, 1973.
      Heidel von Hymack, carrier of every fatal disease known to
      mankind, is pursued by Malacar Miles, Dr. Pels, and Francis
      Sandow, each for his own purpose. Though not published
      until 1973, *Italbar* was written in 1965.

C.   MISCELLANEOUS

85   *The Illustrated Roger Zelazny*. New York: Baronet Press, 1978.
      Illustrated by Gray Morrow. Contains an original story about
      Jack of Shadows called "Shadowjack." It precedes the action
      of *Jack of Shadows*. Also contains illustrated versions of "A
      Rose for Ecclesiastes" and "The Furies," an illustrated adapta-
      tion of "The Doors of His Face, the Lamps of His Mouth,"
      and two illustrated tapestries, one on the Amber novels.

86   "Introduction." In *A Private Cosmos* by Jose Philip Farmer. New
      York: Ace Books, 1976, pp. v-ix.

87   "Introduction." In *From the Land of Fear* by Harlan Ellison. New
      York: Belmont Books, 1967, pp. 7-10.

88   "Science Fiction and How It Got That Way." *The Writer*, May 1971,
      pp. 15-17.

89   "Some Science Fiction Parameters: A Biased Opinion." *Galaxy*,
      July 1975, pp. 6-11.

XII.

SELECTIVELY ANNOTATED
SECONDARY BIBLIGRAPHY

1   Cowper, Richard. "A Rose is a Rose is a Rose ... in Search of
     Richard Zelazny." *Foundation*, No. 11/12 (March 1977), 142-
     147. Cowper asks what happened to the Roger Zelazny who
     wrote "A Rose for Ecclesiastes." He feels that Zelazny has not
     lived up to the promise displayed in his earlier stories. Un-
     fortunately, Cowper's article seems to have been triggered by
     his reading of *To Die in Italbar*, not one of Zelazny's best
     efforts. *Italbar* was originally written in 1965 at a time when
     Zelazny was going through a very difficult personal crisis.
     He only agreed to publish it to fulfill a contract obligation.
     Contrary to speculation, he did not revive Francis Sandow
     from *Isle of the Dead* for this novel. Rather, he extracted
     Sandow from *Italbar* for *Isle of the Dead* because the char-
     acter was one of the few things that he liked about the earlier
     novel.

2   Delany, Samuel R. "Faust and Archimedes." In *Science Fiction
     Writers of America Forum*, 1969, pp. 15-26. Delany compares
     Zelazny and Thomas Disch, discussing their symbolism and
     their impact on science fiction in general.

3   Mebane, Banks. "Gunpowder i' the Court, Wildfire at Midnight."
     Algol, 5, No. 13 (1968), 39-45. Mebane discusses Zelazny's
     stylistic qualities, specifically his figurative language, his
     allusions, his word-play, and his verbal and senuous ideas.

4   Monteleone, Thomas F. "Introduction." In *Isle of the Dead*. Boston:
     Gregg Press, 1976, pp. v-xvi. Monteleone presents an excellent
     analysis of *Isle of the Dead* and marks it as the last major
     statement Zelazny makes about myth. He also presents a
     comprehensive summary of Zelazny's writing career through
     1976.

5   Monteleone, Thomas F. "Fire and Ice—On Roger Zelazny's Short
     Fiction." *Algol*, 13, No. 2 (Summer 1976), 8-14. Monteleone
     reviews briefly "A Rose for Ecclesiastes," "The Doors of His
     Face, the Lamps of His Mouth," "Love is an Imaginary Num-
     ber," "Divine Madness," "The Keys to December," "For A
     Breath I Tarry," and "The Man Who Loved the Faioli."

6   Sanders, Joseph. *Roger Zelazny: A Guide to the Science Fiction*.
     Boston: Gregg Press. To be published early 1979. A bibli-
     ography of works by and about Zelazny.

7   Sanders, Joseph. "Zelazny: Unfinished Business." In *Voices for the
     Future*. Vol. 2. Bowling Green, Ohio: Bowling Green Popular

Press, 1978. Sanders presents an excellent and comprehensive overview of Zelazny's major works.

8   Seavey, Ormond. "Introduction." In *The Dream Master*. Boston: Gregg Press, 1976, pp. v-xiii. Seavey cites as Zelazny's most important quality his confidence that his experimentation with ideas and techniques will work. He feels that *The Dream Master* may be Zelazny's best novel because it deals with personality, a subject that is substantive. He feels that science fiction must deal with serious ideas if it is to be taken seriously.

9   Sturgeon, Theodore. "Introduction." In *Four For Tomorrow*. New York: Ace Books, 1967, pp. 7-13. Sturgeon lavishes praise upon Zelazny and indicates that he will be .a giant among science fiction writers. He does object to what he calls Zelazny's "furniture," that is, obscure allusions, precise German philosophical terms, and mythic citation on the basis that they interfere with the action level of the story.

10   Yoke, Carl B. "Zelazny's *Damnation Alley:* Hell Noh." *Extrapolation*, 15, No. 1 (December 1973), 6-16. A discussion of the noh play that Zelazny added to the shorter version of "Damnation Alley" when he expanded it to novel length and how it raises the level of the story.

INDEX

Absurdity of life, 94, 95
Accelerationism, 62-63, 69
Agni, 66
Alienation, 92, 94, 96
Amber, kingdom of, 79, 81, 82, 83, 84,
  85, 89, 90
Amber novels, The 12, 17, 18, 19, 20,
  80, 86, 87, 88
American Library Association, The, 12
"And Call Me Conrad," 11, 30, 38
"And the Darkness is Harsh," 9
"Angel, Dark Angel," 11
Archetypes, 19, 52
Arthurian lore, 20, 53-54, 81
Auden, John, 96
"Auto-de-Fe," 11
Avalon, kingdom of, 81

Baltimore, Md., 10, 12, 15
Barati, Sanza, 94
Bartelmetz, 51, 55
Belion, 18, 93
"Bells of Shoredan, The," 11
Benedict of Amber, 80
Bible, The, 18, 22
Blake, William, 24, 28
Borel, Lord, 90
"Borgia Hand, The," 10
Borkman, Charles Eliot (the Bork), 95
Brahma. *See* Kali
Brand, 18, 80, 82, 83, 84, 86, 87, 90
Braxa, 20, 22, 23, 24, 25, 26, 27
Bridges of Ashes, 12
Brockden, Jessie, 76, 77, 78
Buddhas, historical, 62, 63, 64, 65, 66
Buddhism, 60, 61, 62, 63, 64, 65, 69, 70
Burns, Manny, 76, 77
"But Not the Herald," 10

Caine of Amber, 90
Callahan, Judith Alene, 11, 15
Camus, Albert, 94
Candi. *See* Kali
Carlyle, Thomas, 35
Carr, Terry, 74
Cassandra, 34, 36, 37
Cassidy, Fred, 96-97
Chaos, the force. *See* Form and Chaos
  philosophy

Chaos, the location, 80, 81, 82, 86, 87,
  88, 89
Chaucer, Geoffrey, 14
Chisel in the Sky, 14
"Circe Has Her Problems," 10
Cleveland, Ohio, 10, 13, 14
"Collector's Fever," 10
Color symbolism, 22, 58
Columbia University, 9, 10, 14
"Come Not to Me In Winter's White," 11
"Comes Now the Power," 11
"Corrida," 11
Corwin of Amber, 18, 19, 20, 80-92,
  passim
Courts of Chaos, The, 12, 15, 21, 80, 81,
  83, 84, 87
Covert, Dick, 9, 14
Crane, Harte, 14
"Creatures of Darkness," 11
"Creatures of Light," 11
Creatures of Light and Darkness, 11

"Damnation Alley," 11
Damnation Alley, 11, 15, 16, 74, 92
Dance as symbol, the, 19, 20, 22, 26-27
Dante, 50, 95
Dara, 80, 82, 86, 90
Dark, Jarry, 16, 93
Da Vinci Syndrome, the, 39
Davits, Carlton, 18, 19, 42-48, *passim*,
  56, 64
"Dawn," 11, 20
"Death and the Executioner," 11
Deicratism, 61, 63, 68, 69
Deicrats, 64, 65, 67
Deidre, of Amber, 80, 84
Denmark, Harrison, 10
Deus Irae, 12
"Devil Car," 10
DeVille, Jill, 52, 54
Devil, the, 34, 87, 88
Diane (Redwig), 31, 35
Dick, Philip K., 12
"Diet," 9
Dilvish, Colonel, 80
Dionysius, 32, 33, 35
"Dismal Light," 11
"Divine Madness," 11
Dolphins, 74, 75

www.ingramcontent.com/pod-product-compliance
Lightning Source LLC
Chambersburg PA
CBHW021343090426
42742CB00008B/729